THE HEINLE
PICTURE
DICTIONARY

Intermediate Workbook

Barbara H. Foley

THOMSON

™

HEINLE

United States ◇ Australia ◇ Canada ◇ Mexico ◇ Singapore ◇ United Kingdom

THOMSON

HEINLE

The Heinle Picture Dictionary
Intermediate Workbook
Barbara H. Foley

Publisher, Adult & Academic: *James W. Brown*
Director of Product Development: *Anita Raducanu*
Executive Editor, Adult & Academic:
   Sherrise Roehr
Publisher, Global ELT: *Christopher Wenger*
Associate Development Editor: *John Hicks*
Editorial Assistant: *Katherine Reilly*
Product Marketing Manager: *Laura Needham*
Field Marketing Manager: *Donna Lee Kennedy*
International Marketing Manager: *Ian Martin*
Director of Product Marketing: *Amy Mabley*

Senior Production Editor: *Maryellen E. Killeen*
Senior Print Buyer: *Mary Beth Hennebury*
Project Management, Design, and Composition:
   InContext Publishing Partners
Cover Design: *InContext Publishing Partners*
Cover Image: *© 2004 Roy Wiemann c/o the ispot.com*
Printer: *Transcontinental*

Printed in Canada.
1 2 3 4 5 6 7 8 9 10   09 08 07 06

For more information contact Thomson Heinle, 25 Thomson Place, Boston, MA 02210 USA, or you can visit our Internet site at elt.thomson.com

For permission to use material from this text or product, submit a request online at
http://www.thomsonrights.com

Any additional questions about permissions can be submitted by email to thomsonrights@thomson.com

Student Edition ISBN: 1-4130-1467-4

International Student Edition ISBN:
1-4130-2231-6 (Not for sale in the United States.)

Credits

Illustrators

Cheryl Kirk Noll/CATugeau LLC: pp. 115–117
Greg LaFever/Scott Hull Associates Inc.: pp. 83 (top), 184, 189
Precision Graphics: pp. 2, 3 (A–D), 55, 169, 175 (top), 193, 207
Susan Spellman/Gwen Walters Artist Representative: pp. 71, 75, 79
Carol Stutz Illustration: pp. 100, 113, 145, 163
Gary Torrisi/Gwen Walters Artist Representative: pp. 12, 81, 120, 130 (bottom), 131
Meryl Treatner/CATugeau LLC: pp. 10 (bottom), 11 (bottom), 108–110, 111 (bottom), 133 (1–3)

Photos

Unit One   UNIT ICON CREDIT: ©Tom Grill/Corbis; 3: ©Hemera Photo-Objects; 4: ©IndexOpen/RF; 7: ©Photos.com/RF; 8: ©Hemera Photo-Objects; 10 (top): ©Photos.com/RF; 11 (top): ©D. Hurst/Alamy; 14 (top 3): ©Photos.com/RF; 14 (bottom 3): ©IndexOpen/RF; 16 (A): ©Royalty-Free/Corbis; 16 (B–F): ©IndexOpen/RF

Unit Two   UNIT ICON CREDIT: ©Royalty-Free/Corbis; 19: ©Photos.com/RF; 21 (1–4): ©Photos.com/RF; 21 (5–6): ©IndexOpen/RF; 22–23: ©IndexOpen/RF; 24: ©Hemera Photo-Objects

Unit Three   UNIT ICON CREDIT: ©Thinkstock/Getty Images; 26 (A): ©IndexOpen/RF; 26 (B–C): ©Photos.com/RF; 27 (top): ©IndexOpen/RF; 28–29: ©IndexOpen/RF; 30 (1–4): ©Photos.com/RF; 30 (5): ©IndexOpen/RF; 31: ©SUNSET BOULEVARD/CORBIS SYGMA

Unit Four   UNIT ICON CREDIT: ©Jose Luis Pelaez, Inc./Corbis; 32: ©Photos.com/RF; 33: ©IndexOpen/RF; 34–35: ©Hemera Photo-Objects; 39: ©Photos.com/RF; 40 (1, 3–5): ©Photos.com/RF; 40 (2, 6): ©IndexOpen/RF; 42 (B 1) ©Photos.com/RF; 42 (B 2–4): ©IndexOpen/RF; 44: ©IndexOpen/RF

Unit Five   UNIT ICON CREDIT: ©Photodisc Collection/Getty Images; 47 (A): ©Photos.com/RF; 47 (B–C): ©IndexOpen/RF; 49 (1): ©Photos.com/RF; 49 (2–6): ©IndexOpen/RF; 53: ©Brand X Pictures; 60: ©IndexOpen/RF

Unit Six   UNIT ICON CREDIT: ©Cydney Conger/Corbis; 62 (1): ©Photos.com/RF; 62 (2, 4–6): ©IndexOpen/RF; 62 (3): ©V&A Images/Alamy; 65: ©IndexOpen/RF; 70: ©Hemera Photo-Objects; 73: ©IndexOpen/RF; 76 (1): ©Hemera Photo-Objects; 76 (2, 6): ©IndexOpen/RF; 76 (3–4, 6): ©Photos.com/RF; 80: ©Hemera Photo-Objects

Unit Seven   UNIT ICON CREDIT: ©Burke-Triolo Productions/Getty Images; 83 (bottom): ©IndexOpen/RF; 84 (1–5, 7–8): ©Hemera Photo-Objects; 85 (C): ©Hemera Photo-Objects; 85 (D 1–7, 9–10): ©Hemera Photo-Objects; 85 (bottom): ©Photos.com/RF; 86 (A): ©Photos.com/RF; 88: ©Hemera Photo-Objects; 89: ©IndexOpen/RF; 90: ©Hemera Photo-Objects; 93 (top): ©Hemera Photo-Objects; 93 (bottom): ©Photos.com/RF; 95–96: ©Hemera Photo-Objects; 98: ©IndexOpen/RF; 101: ©Hemera Photo-Objects; 103 (middle): ©Photos.com/RF; 103 (bottom): ©Hemera Photo-Objects

Unit Eight   UNIT ICON CREDIT: ©C Squared Studios/Getty Images; 104 (1, 3, 5): ©Photos.com/RF; 104 (2, 4, 6): ©IndexOpen/RF; 107: ©Hemera Photo-Objects; 111 (1–2, 4): ©Hemera Photo-Objects; 111 (3): ©Photos.com/RF; 114 (1): ©IndexOpen/RF; 114 (2–4): ©Hemera Photo-Objects

Unit Nine   UNIT ICON CREDIT: ©Wes Thompson/Corbis; 119 (1–10) ©Hemera Photo-Objects; 123: ©Photos.com/RF; 126 (1, 3–5): ©IndexOpen/RF; 126 (2, 6): ©Photos.com/RF; 129 (1): ©Photos.com/RF; 129 (3): ©IndexOpen/RF; 130 (top): ©IndexOpen/RF

Unit Ten   UNIT ICON CREDIT: ©Herrmann/Starke/Corbis; 132: ©IndexOpen/RF; 133 (bottom 1–2): ©Hemera Photo-Objects; 133 (bottom 3): ©IndexOpen/RF; 136: ©Hemera Photo-Objects; 139 (1, 3): ©IndexOpen/RF; 139 (2): ©Photos.com/RF; 140 (1, 3): ©Hemera Photo-Objects; 140 (2, 4, 6): ©IndexOpen/RF; 140 (5): ©Photos.com/RF; 142: ©Hemera Photo-Objects

Unit Eleven   UNIT ICON CREDIT: ©PictureNet/Corbis; 146: ©Hemera Photo-Objects; 150 (1, 3, 5–8): ©IndexOpen/RF; 150 (2, 4): ©Photos.com/RF; 152: ©Hemera Photo-Objects; 155: ©IndexOpen/RF; 156–158: ©Hemera Photo-Objects; 160 (1–2, 4–8): ©Hemera Photo-Objects; 160 (3): ©IndexOpen/RF; 161: ©Hemera Photo-Objects; 164 (1–3, 5–8): ©Hemera Photo-Objects; 164 (4): ©IndexOpen/RF; 165: ©IndexOpen/RF

Unit Twelve   UNIT ICON CREDIT: ©L. Clarke/Corbis; 167: ©IndexOpen/RF; 168 (1, 4–6, 8): ©Photos.com/RF; 168 (2–3, 7): ©IndexOpen/RF; 170 (1–4, 6): ©Photos.com/RF; 170 (5): ©IndexOpen/RF; 171 (A–B): ©IndexOpen/RF; 171 (C): ©Photos.com/RF; 173: (1–5): IndexOpen/RF; 173 (6): ©Photos.com/RF; 175 (1–2, 4–6): ©IndexOpen/RF; 175 (3): ©Photos.com/RF; 176: ©IndexOpen/RF

Unit Thirteen   UNIT ICON CREDIT: ©Digital Vision/Getty Images; 179: ©Hemera Photo-Objects; 181 (top): ©IndexOpen/RF; 181 (bottom): ©Hemera Photo-Objects; 182: ©Hemera Photo-Objects; 183 (1, 3–5): ©Hemera Photo-Objects; 183 (2): ©Paul Springett/Alamy; 183 (6): ©Royalty-Free/Corbis; 187 (middle): ©Hemera Photo-Objects; 187 (A): ©IndexOpen/RF; 187 (B–D): ©Photos.com/RF; 188 (1, 6–7): ©Photos.com/RF; 188 (2–5, 8): ©IndexOpen/RF; 190 (1–5, 8–12): ©Photos.com/RF; 190 (6): ©Daniel Dempster Photography/Alamy; 190 (7): ©IndexOpen/RF; 191: ©Hemera Photo-Objects

Unit Fourteen   UNIT ICON CREDIT: ©Don Farrall/Getty Images; 192: ©IndexOpen/RF; 194: (2, 4–6): ©IndexOpen/RF; 194 (1, 3): ©Photos.com/RF; 195 (A–E): ©Hemera Photo-Objects; 199 (A, C–D): ©Photos.com/RF; 199 (B, F–H): ©IndexOpen/RF; 199 (E): ©Andrew K/epa/epa/Corbis; 200 (A, C): ©Bettmann/CORBIS; 200 (B): ©CORBIS; 200 (D): ©Christopher J. Morris/CORBIS

Unit Fifteen   UNIT ICON CREDIT: ©Don Farrall/Getty Images; 203 (1, 3–4): ©Photos.com/RF; 203 (2): ©IndexOpen/RF; 205: ©IndexOpen/RF; 206 (1–2): ©Photos.com/RF; 106 (3–6): ©IndexOpen/RF; 208 (1–4, 6): ©IndexOpen/RF; 208 (5): ©Photos.com/RF

Unit Sixteen   UNIT ICON CREDIT: ©Digital Vision/Getty Images; 210: ©IndexOpen/RF; 211 (1–2, 4–6): ©IndexOpen/RF; 211(3): ©Photos.com/RF; 212: ©Hemera Photo-Objects; 213: ©IndexOpen/RF; 215: ©IndexOpen/RF; 216 (1–7): ©Hemera Photo-Objects; 216 (8): ©IndexOpen/RF; 218 (1): ©PhotoAlto/Alamy; 218 (2–6): ©Hemera Photo-Objects; 219–220: ©Hemera Photo-Objects; 221: ©IndexOpen/RF; 222: ©Hemera Photo-Objects; 223: ©IndexOpen/RF; 224 (1, 3–6): ©Hemera Photo-Objects; 224 (2): ©IndexOpen/RF; 225 (1, 3–4, 6): ©IndexOpen/RF; 225 (2): ©Photos.com/RF; 225 (A–G): ©Hemera Photo-Objects; 226: ©IndexOpen/RF; 227 (1): ©Judith Collins/Alamy; 227 (2, 5): ©Photos.com/RF; 227 (3–4, 6): ©IndexOpen/RF; 228 (1–2, 4): ©Photos.com/RF; 228 (3): ©IndexOpen/RF

To the Teacher

The Heinle Picture Dictionary Intermediate Workbook provides intermediate students with a variety of activities to practice and reinforce the vocabulary learned in *The Heinle Picture Dictionary*. The workbook can be used in conjunction with class instruction or can be used on its own.

The workbook follows the same page-by-page format as *The Heinle Picture Dictionary*. For example, after introducing a spread such as City Square (pages 58–59) in the dictionary, students can complete the corresponding pages in the workbook (pages 58–59). The exercises can be done in class, in small groups, or assigned as homework.

The workbook offers a wide variety of vocabulary practice activities. Some are at the word level, for example, asking students to choose words that can follow a particular verb, selecting the two words with similar meanings, or placing words in categories. Most activities are at the sentence level. Students may write the correct vocabulary word in sentences, place steps in order, decide if statements are true or false, or decide if sentences are the same or different in meaning. In many activities, students write the correct response to questions or comments about the topic. Students are often asked to write sentences in their notebooks based on colorful, attractive photographs or illustrations related to the vocabulary topic. Each unit ends with a *Word Work* activity. Though these exercises may be done individually, they are best accomplished in a small group or with a partner. Using the vocabulary in the unit, students discuss and compare their experiences, preferences, area highlights, similarities and differences, favorite recipes, schedules, etc.

A unique and important feature of this workbook is the listening activity that appears in each lesson. The listening activities reinforce the vocabulary in a number of ways. Many listening exercises ask the students to match pictures with sentences or short dialogues. Students might hear sentences about a picture and decide if they are true or false. In other listening activities, students answer questions about conversations, circle the correct response, identify the correct person, write prices, or follow directions. There is ample support for the listening exercises, with pictures and word boxes providing spelling assistance. It will be necessary to pause between each item in the listening exercises to allow students sufficient time to choose the correct answer. Students often find it helpful to listen to the exercises more than once. When the listening activity is done in class, students should be encouraged to listen to the CD again at home for review.

The final page of each workbook unit provides a *Word Study* box. These are vocabulary learning strategies. Learners need several exposures to a new word or phrase in order to learn it. Short practice periods with frequent review are usually more effective than long study sessions. Teachers can introduce the strategies at any time and in any order. Allow class time in which to discuss the ideas and get student feedback. Some students may have additional helpful strategies to offer the class. Students should identify two or three strategies that are effective for them. Time spent in class reflecting on how to study can help students acquire more effective learning strategies.

Many students find that a personal vocabulary notebook helps them record new words and allows for quick review sessions. A sample page from such a notebook and additional suggestions for choosing and recording new words are presented on the next page.

Enjoy using *The Heinle Picture Dictionary Workbook* in your class and watching your students' vocabulary grow!

A Vocabulary Notebook

Many students find that a vocabulary notebook is a helpful way to learn and review new vocabulary words. The sample below shows part of a vocabulary notebook page.

bald - no hair

glasses

moustache

get on (the bus)

cross (the street)

fall - caer

leave - dejar

angry

thirsty - I am thirsty. I'd like a soda.

love -

worried - preocupado

brush your teeth

comb your hair

put on makeup - maquillarse

take a nap - short sleep in the daytime

do housework - hacer las tareas de la casa

What words should I put in my vocabulary notebook?

This is *your* personal notebook. Put in words *you* want to remember. Write some new words from your dictionary. Add words that you see or hear in school or at work. Write words that you hear on TV or in a song you like.

How should I write the words?

Students write new words in different ways. Sometimes, you will remember the word when you see it. For other words, you can translate the word into your own language or draw a simple picture. You may also want to write a short sentence with the word or write a definition.

How can I learn new words?

There are three rules for learning new vocabulary:

Rule #1: Review.

Rule #2: Review.

Rule #3: Review again.

Contents

15 The Arts

16 Recreation

Numbers

A **Write the number.**

a. 9 ___nine___

b. 14 _____

c. 19 _____

d. 25 _____

e. 38 _____

f. 43 _____

g. 57 _____

h. 60 _____

i. 72 _____

j. 81 _____

k. 96 _____

l. 100 _____

B **Write the age of each person on his/her next birthday.**

1. I'm nine. I'm going to be ___ten___.

2. I'm twelve. I'm going to be _____.

3. I'm seventeen. I'll be _____.

4. I'm twenty. I'll be _____.

5. I'm twenty-nine. I'm going to be _____.

6. I'm thirty-two. I'm going to be _____.

7. I'm fifty-seven. I'll be _____.

8. I'm sixty-four. I'm going to be _____.

CD 1
Track 1

C **Listen and circle the letter of the correct floor.**

1. **(a.)** It's on the first floor.   **b.** It's on the fifth floor.

2. **a.** It's on the second floor.   **b.** It's on the third floor.

3. **a.** It's on the eighth floor.   **b.** It's on the ninth floor.

4. **a.** It's on the sixth floor.   **b.** It's on the seventh floor.

5. **a.** It's on the fourth floor.   **b.** It's on the fifth floor.

6. **a.** It's on the third floor.   **b.** It's on the tenth floor.

7. **a.** It's on the third floor.   **b.** It's on the fourth floor.

8. **a.** It's on the second floor.   **b.** It's on the sixth floor.

Floor	Tenant
10	Radio Station
9	Dr. Garcia
8	CompCo
7	Tax Office
6	Prime Paints
5	Dr. Blackman
4	Couseling Center
3	Law Office
2	Art School
1	Dr. Chan

D Match the statement with the correct chart.

1. Three quarters of the students are studying English. _c_

2. Half of the students are studying English. ____

3. One quarter of the students are studying English. ____

4. Two thirds of the students are studying English. ____

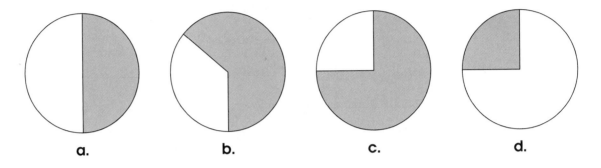

a.   b.   c.   d.

CD 1
Track 2

E Listen and complete the forms.

Name: _____ Jiang Xu _____

Student ID: _____

Cell Phone: _____

Name: _____ Julia Hernandez _____

Student ID: _____

Telephone Number: _____

Word Work **Small Group**

Write or discuss. Use numbers in your answers.

1. What is the address of your school?

2. How many floors are in your school building?

3. What floor is your classroom on?

4. What is your classroom number?

5. How many students are in your class? How many men? How many women?

6. About how many students are in your school?

Time

A Match.

_c_	1. a minute	a.	100 years
___	2. an hour	b.	365 days
___	3. a day	c.	60 seconds
___	4. a week	d.	24 hours
___	5. a month	e.	7 days
___	6. a year	f.	60 minutes
___	7. a decade	g.	1,000 years
___	8. a century	h.	28–31 days
___	9. a millennium	i.	10 years

CD 1
Track 3

B Listen and fill in the correct times.

1.
Bank
_9_ : _00_ to ___:___

2.
Library
___:___ to ___:___

3.
Restaurant
___:___ to ___:___

4.
Supermarket
___:___ to ___:___

5.
Post Office
___:___ to ___:___

6.
Barbershop
___:___ to ___:___

C Circle the time that is later.

1. a. six fifteen   (b.) six thirty

2. a. five past three   b. three ten

3. a. four thirty   b. a quarter past four

4. a. ten to eight   b. seven forty-five

5. a. two twenty-five   b. two thirty

6. a. nine forty   b. a quarter to ten

7. a. eleven ten   b. five past eleven

8. a. seven fifteen   b. twenty after seven

D Write the correct preposition, *at* or *in*.

1. I get up __at__ seven o'clock.

2. I take the bus to school ____ the morning.

3. I eat lunch ____ noon.

4. School ends ____ 2:00.

5. I do my homework ____ the evening.

6. I watch my favorite TV show ____ 9:00.

7. I use my computer ____ night.

8. I go to bed ____ midnight.

at
at 5:00
at seven o'clock
at noon
at night
at midnight

in
in the morning
in the afternoon
in the evening

E Complete this information about yourself. Write the number of minutes, days, hours, weeks, months, or years for each sentence.

1. It takes me _____ to get to school.

2. I study vocabulary for _____ every day.

3. I sleep _____ a night.

4. I watch TV _____ a day.

5. I have _____ vacation from work/school.

6. I have been absent from school _____ this year.

7. I talk on the phone _____ a day.

8. I go to school _____ a week.

9. I have been studying English for _____ .

Word Work **Small Group**

Answer each question. Then, discuss your answers with your group. Complete the sentences.

1. What time do you get up? _____   _____ gets up the earliest.

2. What time do you go to bed? _____   _____ goes to bed the latest.

3. What hours do you work? _____   _____ works the most hours.

4. What hours do you sleep? _____   _____ sleeps the longest.

Calendar

A **Write the day for each abbreviation.**

1. Tues. _____Tuesday_____

2. Fri. _____

3. Sun. _____

4. Mon. _____

5. Wed. _____

6. Sat. _____

7. Thurs. _____

B **Write the next month.**

1. February _____March_____

2. May _____

3. October _____

4. August _____

5. December _____

6. April _____

7. January _____

8. June _____

C **Complete the sentence with the name of a month.**

1. I usually go on vacation in _____.

2. My birthday is in _____.

3. New Year's Day is in _____.

4. People celebrate Christmas in _____.

5. School begins in _____ and ends in _____.

6. _____ is the coldest month of the year.

7. _____ is the hottest month of the year.

8. _____ is my favorite month.

D **Write the date. Use this form: month/day/year.**

1. February 22, 2004 ___2/22/2004___

2. May 4, 1997 _____

3. October 15, 1950 _____

4. March 14, 2005 _____

5. July 1, 2006 _____

6. December 10, 2001 _____

7. August 18, 1948 _____

8. January 7, 2010 _____

E Look at the Word Partnerships Box on page 7 of the dictionary. Write the correct preposition, *in* or *on*.

1. I got my driver's license __in__ May.

2. I have a doctor's appointment ____ Tuesday.

3. We don't have school ____ the summer.

4. I got married ____ June 21st.

5. My birthday is ____ November.

6. I don't work ____ Sunday.

7. It's very cold ____ the winter.

8. My vacation begins ____ August 1st.

9. School begins ____ September.

10. We have a test ____ Monday.

CD 1
Track 4

F Listen and write the month of each holiday from around the world.

1. Japan celebrates Tanabata on _____ 7th.

2. In India, people celebrate Diwali in _____ .

3. New Year's is usually in _____ in China.

4. Cinco de Mayo on _____ 5th
   is a popular holiday in Mexico.

5. _____ 13th is Santa Lucia,
   a national holiday in Sweden.

6. South Africa celebrates National Woman's Day
   on _____ 9th.

7. _____ 23rd is Children's Day in Turkey.

Word Work Small Group

Write three dates that are important in your life, such as your birthday, anniversary, a graduation, etc. Read the dates to your classmates. Explain why each date is important to you.

1. _____   2. _____   3. _____

Money and Shopping

A **Match the amounts.**

   _c_   **1.** two nickels   **a.** a quarter

         2. five pennies   **b.** twenty cents

         3. two dimes and one nickel   **c.** a dime

         4. four quarters   **d.** forty cents

         5. four nickels   **e.** a nickel

         6. two quarters   **f.** fifty cents

         7. four dimes   **g.** thirty cents

         8. one quarter and one nickel   **h.** a dollar

B **Write the coins and bills each person will receive as change.**

1. Joseph buys a stamp for forty cents. He gives the clerk a dollar.

    Change: _a dime and two quarters_ _____

2. Ana buys a cup of coffee for $1.20. She gives the clerk $1.50.

    Change: _____

3. Hoang buys a notebook for $3.79. He gives the clerk five dollars.

    Change: _____

4. Raj buys a CD for $12.60. He gives the clerk twenty dollars.

    Change: _____

CD 1
Track 5

C **Write the price of each item.**

   $1.00 _____

D Complete the conversation between the cashier and the shopper on page 9 of the dictionary. Write the correct answer after each question.

It's $1.45.	Yes, but you need your receipt.
The regular price is $36.00.	The sale price is $27.00.
~~Yes, they are.~~	No, we only accept cash and credit cards.

1. Are these hats on sale today?

   Yes, they are.

2. How much is this hat?

3. How much is the sale price?

4. How much is the sales tax?

5. Can I pay by check?

6. Can I return the hat?

Word Work Small Group

Are you a smart shopper? Circle *yes* or *no* for each statement. Then, discuss each item with your group. Which students in your group are smart shoppers?

1.	I try to buy things on sale.	Yes	No
2.	I always check my receipt.	Yes	No
3.	I always keep my receipt.	Yes	No
4.	I have one or two credit cards.	Yes	No
5.	I always pay with cash.	Yes	No
6.	I check the prices in two or three stores.	Yes	No

Colors

A **Write the names of the colors you see in each picture.**

1. The colors in the picture of the hot air balloon are _red,_ _____

_____.

2. The colors in the picture of the parrot are _____.

B **Laura is trying to decide which colors to paint her house.**
Write the name of each color. Check the house you like best.

Shutters

___   ___   ___

House:_____   House:_____   House:_____

Shutters:_____   Shutters:_____   Shutters:_____

Door:_____   Door:_____   Door:_____

C **Complete the sentences with color words.**

1. The flag of my country is _____.

2. A stop sign is _____.

3. A traffic light is _____.

4. A fire engine is _____.

5. A police car is _____.

6. A fire hydrant is _____.

7. A school bus is _____.

8. An ambulance is _____.

9. An airplane is usually _____.

10. A taxi is usually _____.

CD 1
Track 6

D **Listen to the description of each boy's clothing. Write each name under the correct boy.**

| Ben | Jesse | Jason | Todd | Sam | Kyle |

_____

Ben _____

_____

Word Work **Small Group**

Complete the sentences. Then, read your sentences to one another. What information is the same? What information is different?

1. At a wedding, the bride usually wears a _____ dress.

2. At a funeral, people often wear _____.

3. The _____ is my favorite sports team. They wear _____ uniforms.

4. The clothes I am wearing now are _____.

5. I look good in _____.

6. _____ is my favorite color.

11

In, On, Under

A Complete these sentences with the correct prepositions.

1. There are nine cars _____ *on* _____ the truck.

2. The white car is _____ the red car and the silver car.

3. The red car is _____ the white car.

4. The silver car is _____ the white car.

5. The green car is _____ the silver car.

6. The blue car is _____ the black car.

7. The black car is _____ the sports car.

8. The sports car has a ribbon _____ it.

9. One man is driving the brown car _____ the truck.

10. The woman is standing _____ the truck.

11. The two men are _____ the truck.

12. The cat is _____ the truck.

B Read the description of a bookcase. On a separate piece of paper, draw the bookcase. Then, draw each item.

I have a small bookcase in my room. On top of the bookcase, there is an alarm clock on the right. My camera is on the left. On the top shelf, there are two photographs of my family on the left. On the right, there is a box with lots more photographs inside. My stereo is on the middle shelf. There are lots of CDs beside the stereo. On the bottom shelf, there are some books. Next to the books is a box of tissues. I have two speakers for my stereo. One is to the right of the bookcase and the other is to the left.

C Write seven statements about this desk. Use seven different prepositions.

1. _____
2. _____
3. _____
4. _____
5. _____
6. _____
7. _____

CD 1
Track 7

D Listen to each statement about the desk. Circle *True* or *False*.

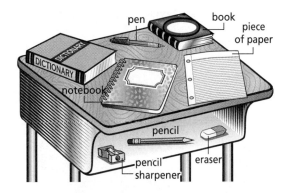

1. True (False)   4. True   False   7. True   False

2. True   False   5. True   False   8. True   False

3. True   False   6. True   False   9. True   False

Word Work **Small Group**

Take out several items from your pockets and backpacks, such as a cell phone, car keys, pen, etc. Arrange the items on the desk. Write seven sentences with prepositions describing the location of each item.

Opposites

A **Circle the correct adjective.**

1. It's (hot (cold)) out today.

2. The boy is wearing a (light   heavy) coat.

3. The traffic is (light   heavy) in the morning.

4. It's a (fast   slow) drive to work.

5. It's often very (noisy   quiet) on the highway.

6. This house is (large   small).

7. It's very (cheap   expensive).

8. If you are (rich   poor), you can buy this house.

B **Write two sentences about each picture. Use the new words in your dictionary.**

1.

2.

3.

1. _____

2. _____

3. _____

C Complete the sentences.

~~difficult~~	loud	hard	hot	full
young	weak	slow	short	

1. I don't understand the math problem. It's too _____difficult_____.

2. I can't reach the top shelf. I'm too _____.

3. Don't eat the soup yet. It's too _____.

4. He won't win the race. He's too _____.

5. She's only fourteen. She's too _____ to drive.

6. I can't eat any more pizza. I'm too _____.

7. This pillow isn't comfortable. It's too _____.

8. My grandmother can't pick up the box. She's too _____.

9. Turn down the radio. It's too _____.

CD 1
Track 8

D Listen and circle the letter of the correct sentence.

1. (a.) She's young.   b. She's old.

2. a. It's full.   b. It's empty.

3. a. She's weak.   b. She's strong.

4. a. It's cold.   b. It's hot.

5. a. It's noisy.   b. It's quiet.

6. a. It's new.   b. It's old.

7. a. They're clean.   b. They're dirty.

8. a. He's poor.   b. He's rich.

Word Work Small Group

Complete the sentences with adjectives. Talk about your answers with your group.
1. I prefer _____ weather.
2. I prefer to live in a _____ _____ area.
3. I prefer a _____ chair.
4. I prefer to marry a _____ _____ man/woman.

The Telephone

a.

b.

c.

d.

e.

f.

1. This person is holding a telephone book.   _c_

2. This person is dialing a number.   ____

3. This person is using a phone card.   ____

4. This person is talking on a cell phone.   ____

5. This person is using a pay phone.   ____

6. This person is hanging up the telephone.   ____

7. This person is wearing a headset.   ____

B **What is each person going to do?**

1. Jason doesn't know the phone number.

   He's going to look it up in the ____phone book____.

2. Marcus can't find the telephone book. He's going to call _____.

3. Christina wants to talk on the phone in her car, but she needs two hands on the wheel. She's going to use a _____.

4. Paula just saw an accident. She's going to call _____.

5. Lynn doesn't need coins to use the pay phone. She's going to use a _____.

6. The phone is ringing. Tom is going to _____ it.

C **Match the questions and the answers.**

_b_ **1.** What's the number for emergency assistance?   **a.** $5, $10, or $20

____ **2.** What's the number for information?   **b.** 911

____ **3.** How many time zones are there in the United States?   **c.** 305

____ **4.** What's your telephone number?   **d.** 30 cents

____ **5.** What's the area code for Miami?   **e.** 411

____ **6.** How much is a local call?   **f.** 555-4545

____ **7.** How much is a calling card?   **g.** four

CD 1
Track 9

D **Listen to each sound or speaker. What is happening? Write the number of each sound or speaker next to the correct sentence.**

____ **a.** The phone is ringing.

____ **b.** She's answering the phone.

_1_ **c.** She's dialing a number.

____ **d.** She's making an international call.

____ **e.** She's putting coins in a pay phone.

____ **f.** She's asking for directory assistance.

____ **g.** She's leaving a message on an answering machine.

Word Study

There are many ways to study new vocabulary words. Some students learn by writing, some students say the words out loud, some students like to use an audio CD and repeat words, and other students study with a partner. How do you learn new words? Listen to other students give suggestions. Try several different methods.

Classroom

A Look at the classroom on page 18 in your dictionary. Circle *T* if the statement is true. Circle *F* if the statement is false.

1. There are twelve students in this class.   T   (F)
2. The clock is over the blackboard.   T   F
3. The homework assignment is on the whiteboard.   T   F
4. The man in the red shirt has a good grade.   T   F
5. Two students are looking at the map.   T   F
6. The teacher is using the overhead projector.   T   F
7. There are several flags on the bulletin board.   T   F
8. One student has a tape recorder on her desk.   T   F

B Complete the sentences.

1. She listened to a story on the _____ tape recorder _____.
2. For your _____, please complete pages 18 and 19.
3. A _____ is round. It shows the countries of the world.
4. You write on a whiteboard with a _____.
5. You write on a blackboard with _____.
6. His _____ on the test was 90%.
7. Study hard. We have a big _____ tomorrow.
8. Please put the book on the _____.

C Complete the sentences.

high school   college   ~~international~~   graduate

1. An _____ international _____ student is a student from another country.
2. A _____ student is often between the ages of 18 and

22 years old. He chooses a major such as business, art, or science.

3. A _____ student is usually between 14 and 18 years

old. She usually lives at home with her parents.

4. A _____ student continues to study after college.

D Write the sentence with a similar meaning.

> She failed the test.
> She studied for the test.
> She cheated on the test.
> She took a test.
> ~~She passed the test.~~

1. She got 100% on her test.   _____She passed the test._____

2. She got 55% on her test.   _____

3. She copied from another student. _____

4. She looked at her notes carefully. _____

5. She had an exam.   _____

CD 1
Track 10

E Listen and write the number of each question before the correct answer.

_____ **a.** Let's look at a map.

_____ **b.** Her name is Ms. Jackson.

_____ **c.** I got an A.

_____ **d.** It's on the bookcase.

_____ **e.** I don't know. There's a clock in the classroom.

_____ **f.** Do pages 18 and 19 in your workbook.

__1__ **g.** It's on the blackboard.

Word Work **Small Group**

Write the names of ten items in your classroom.
Write a sentence describing the location of each item.
    Examples: **The clock is over the door.**
              The blackboard is in front of the classroom.

Listen, Read, Write

A Write a sentence that has the same meaning.

discuss	raise	~~hand out~~
hand in	copy	look up

1. Give the papers to the students. ___ Hand out the papers. _____

2. Find the word in the dictionary. _____

3. Write this sentence. _____

4. Put up your hand. _____

5. Talk about your ideas. _____

6. Give me your papers. _____

B Circle the two words that can follow each verb.

1. hand out: (the books) (the papers) the sentence

2. copy: the word the group the sentence

3. write: the dictionary your name your answer

4. spell: the sentence the word your name

5. talk with: your book your group your partner

6. erase: the board the word the pencil

C Follow the directions.

1. Underline the correct answer.

   10 + 20 =   10   20   <u>30</u>

2. Cross out the wrong answers.

   5 + 5 + 7 =   10   17   27

3. Fill in the blank.

   15 − 5 = ___

4. Circle the correct answer.

   4 + 15 =   11   18   19

5. Darken the correct oval.

   11 + 12 =   ○ 23   ○ 24   ○ 25

6. Check the correct answer.

   12 + 9 =   ___ 20   ___ 21   ___ 22

CD 1
Track 11

D **Listen and write the directions you hear.**

1. _____ *Open your books to page 21.* _____

2. _____

3. _____

4. _____

5. _____

6. _____

7. _____

E **Look at the classroom pictures. On another piece of paper, write about each picture. Describe what the students are doing.**

Word Work **Partners**

How do you like to study a new language? Check the activities that you find helpful.
Compare your answers with your partner's.

☐ **1.** I like to write sentences.

☐ **2.** I like to copy new words.

☐ **3.** I like to listen to the new language.

☐ **4.** I like to talk with a group.

☐ **5.** I like to read in the new language.

☐ **6.** I like to look up new words in the dictionary.

☐ **7.** I like to do exercises, such as fill-in and matching.

☐ **8.** I like to _____ .

School

A **Match the student and the location.**

<u>d</u> **1.** He feels sick.

_____ **2.** He is listening to Spanish cassettes.

_____ **3.** He is eating lunch.

_____ **4.** He is practicing for the graduation ceremony.

_____ **5.** He is changing his schedule.

_____ **6.** He is taking an English class.

_____ **7.** He is writing a report.

_____ **8.** He is playing basketball.

a. auditorium

b. cafeteria

c. classroom

d. nurse's office

e. gym

f. library

g. language lab

h. guidance office

B **Write the correct person.**

1. This person manages a school. _____ *a principal* _____

2. This person calls a parent when a child is sick. _____

3. This person helps students plan their schedules. _____

4. This person manages a sports team. _____

5. These students play a sport together. _____

C **Complete these school words.**

1. permission _____

2. language _____

3. water _____

4. absence _____

5. guidance _____

6. report _____

7. teachers' _____

D **Complete the sentences.**

1. The principal makes the announcements

   on the ___loudspeaker___ .

2. A _____ shows a student's classes, with

   the days and times.

3. When a child is sick, a parent writes an _____ .

4. Students carry their books to school in _____ .

5. Students sit on _____ to watch sports in the gym.

6. A parent signs a _____ to allow a child to go on a class trip.

7. Students keep their coats and books in their _____ .

8. A _____ gives a student's grades in each subject.

9. Students who live far from school take the _____ .

10. Students listen to speakers and watch movies in the _____ .

CD 1
Track 12

E **Listen to each statement. Where is each student?**

1. _____cafeteria_____

2. _____

3. _____

4. _____

5. _____

6. _____

7. _____

8. _____

9. _____

Word Work **Partners**

Write your school schedule. How is your schedule the
same as your partner's? How is it different?

Computers

A **Write the name of each computer component.**

1. _a laptop_   2. _____   3. _____   4. _____

5. _____   6. _____   7. _____   8. _____

B **Write the correct word.**

a handheld	~~a disk~~	a mouse
a keyboard	an e-mail message	the Internet
a mouse pad	a cable	a printer

1. You can save a lot of information on it.   _____a disk_____

2. You type on it.   _____

3. You can print a report on it.   _____

4. A friend sends it to you.   _____

5. It moves the cursor.   _____

6. Your mouse sits on it.   _____

7. It connects computers around the world.   _____

8. You can carry this computer in your pocket.   _____

9. It connects a printer to a computer.   _____

C   Cross out the word that does not belong.

1. **a.** CD-ROM   **b.** ~~toolbar~~   **c.** disk

2. **a.** cable   **b.** file   **c.** folder

3. **a.** laptop   **b.** desktop   **c.** an e-mail

4. **a.** mouse   **b.** scanner   **c.** mouse pad

5. **a.** projector   **b.** keyboard   **c.** key

6. **a.** monitor   **b.** screen   **c.** printer

D   Read each instruction. Is it possible or impossible?

	Possible	Impossible
1. Put a monitor into the CD-ROM drive.	____	✓
2. Print a scroll bar on the projector.	____	____
3. Move the cursor with a mouse.	____	____
4. Click on an icon.	____	____
5. Scan a picture on the keyboard.	____	____
6. Surf the scanner.	____	____
7. Delete a mouse pad.	____	____
8. Connect to the Internet from your house.	____	____

E   Listen and complete the directions.

CD 1
Track 13

1. Press a _____ .

2. Send an _____ .

3. _____ on an icon.

4. _____ the text.

5. Open a _____ .

6. _____ a picture.

7. Insert a _____ .

8. _____ your password.

9. Surf the _____ .

10. Attach the _____ .

Word Study

Study vocabulary for short periods of time, for example, ten minutes twice a day. The more frequently you see and practice a word, the more likely you are to remember it.

Family

a.

b.

c.

A **A family member is describing his/her family. Choose the picture that shows his/her family.**

1. I'm a single father.   _a_

2. I have four sisters.   ____

3. I live with my grandmother and grandfather.   ____

4. We have two daughters.   ____

5. My mother-in-law is helpful with the children. ____

6. I have two brothers and three sisters.   ____

7. My parents live with my wife and me.   ____

8. We have two children.   ____ and ____

9. I have an older brother.   ____ and ____

10. We have one son.   ____

B **Write the relationship.**

1. My mother's brother is my _____ uncle _____.

2. My mother's sister is my _____.

3. My mother's father is my _____.

4. My brother's wife is my _____.

5. My sister's husband is my _____.

6. My brother's daughter is my _____.

C. Read the information about the family. Then, match the relationships.

Tammy Katie Jack Emma

Mike

Jack and Sylvia were married for three years. They had a boy, Mike. Jack and Sylvia got divorced. Jack remarried, and his second wife's name is Katie. Jack and Katie have two little girls, Emma and Tammy.

___b___ 1. Sylvia and Jack are

_____ 2. Sylvia is Jack's

_____ 3. Jack has three

_____ 4. Jack has two

_____ 5. Emma and Tammy are Mike's

_____ 6. Mike is Katie's

_____ 7. Katie is Mike's

a. half sisters.

b. divorced.

c. daughters.

d. ex-wife.

e. stepmother.

f. stepson.

g. children.

CD 1
Track 14

D. Listen and write the name of the correct person.

Hiro
Masa Yoko Julia Loretta

Eddie Yoshiko

1. _____Julia_____

2. _____

3. _____

4. _____

5. _____

6. _____

7. _____

Word Work   Group

Complete the information about your family in the yellow box. Share the information with your group and complete the information in the pink box.

1. I have ____ brothers.

2. I have ____ sisters.

3. I have ____ aunts.

4. I have ____ uncles.

1. Who has the most brothers? _____

2. Who has the most sisters? _____

3. Who has the most aunts? _____

4. Who has the most uncles? _____

27

Raising a Child

A **Match the sentences with similar meanings.**

__c__ **1.** She's putting a clean diaper on him.

_____ **2.** She's putting on his clothes.

_____ **3.** She's giving him a bottle.

_____ **4.** She's driving him to school.

_____ **5.** She's washing his hair.

_____ **6.** She's getting him after school.

_____ **7.** She's saying good-night.

a. She's picking him up.

b. She's putting him to bed.

c. She's changing him.

d. She's feeding him.

e. She's dressing him.

f. She's dropping him off.

g. She's bathing him.

B **Circle the letter of the sentence that gives an example of each request.**

1. Praise her: **(a.)** That's a beautiful picture. **b.** Let's go to the library.

2. Discipline her: **a.** Don't play with the ball inside. **b.** It's time for dinner.

3. Protect her: **a.** You can't go to the park alone. **b.** Do your homework now.

4. Encourage her: **a.** It's time to go to bed. **b.** I know you can do it.

5. Help her: **a.** Let's do your math homework. **b.** You are growing up.

6. Comfort her: **a.** Come on. Time for your bath. **b.** Don't worry. It's okay.

7. Love her: **a.** Are you ready for school? **b.** You are so special.

C **Listen and write the number of each statement next to the correct request.**

CD 1
Track 15

_____ **a.** Please change him.

__1__ **b.** Please feed him.

_____ **c.** Please read to him.

_____ **d.** Please carry him.

_____ **e.** Please discipline him.

_____ **f.** Please put him to bed.

_____ **g.** Please drop him off.

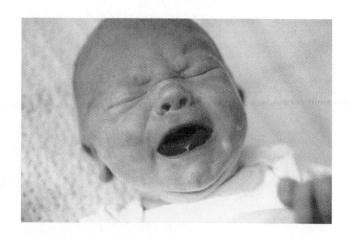

D Write about each picture. What is each parent doing?

1.
2.
3.
4.
5.
6.

1. _____ She's reading a story to her little boy. _____

2. _____

3. _____

4. _____

5. _____

6. _____

Word Work **Partners**

Complete these sentences about yourself. Then, read your sentences to a partner.
1. My parents sometimes played _____ with me.
2. My parents encouraged me to _____.
3. My parents comforted me when I _____.
4. My parents disciplined me when I _____.
5. My parents helped me _____.

Life Events

A **Circle the correct verb.**

Tom ((graduated) celebrated) from college five years ago with a degree in business. He (got   became) a job at a large accounting firm in the city. He (fell   dated) a few young women at his company, but they never became serious. For two years after college, Tom lived at home. Then, he (traveled   rented) an apartment in the city. The first day in his apartment, Tom met Kara, a young woman who lived in the apartment across the hall. They (got   fell) in love and (got   started) engaged a few months later. They (became   got) married a year later. Kara (was   had) soon pregnant and (had   got) twins the following year. Tom and Kara (had   bought) a house a few miles from the city. They need the room. Kara (is   had) pregnant again!

B **Complete the sentences about the pictures using the future tense.**

1.   **2.**   **3.**   **4.**   **5.**

1. After he gets a job, _____ *he's going to get engaged* _____ .

2. After she graduates from college, _____ .

3. After they get married, _____ .

4. After they have a baby, _____ .

5. After she retires, she _____ .

C **Complete the sentences. Be careful of the tense.**

1. Children _____ *start* _____ school when they are five or six years old.

2. Marie and Joseph _____ for six months, but they didn't fall in love.

3. It is expensive to _____ a large family.

4. When Paul _____ sick, he missed two weeks of work.

5. My grandmother is going to _____ her 80th birthday on June 1st.

6. My neighbor _____ in a terrible car accident.

30

D Listen and write the number of each statement or question next to the correct event.

_____ **a.** She had a baby.

_____ **e.** He got sick.

_____ **b.** They bought a house.

_____ **f.** They are going to get married.

__1__ **c.** He got a job.

_____ **g.** They are going to travel.

_____ **d.** She went to college.

_____ **h.** They are going to retire.

E Read about the life of Elvis Presley. Then, complete the time line.

Elvis Presley is known as the King of Rock and Roll. He was born in Mississippi on January 8, 1935. He received his first guitar in 1946. When Elvis was 12, his family moved to Memphis, Tennessee.

Elvis began a career in music. In 1955, he signed a contract with RCA records. He soon became famous for his music, and he acted in several movies. He continued to sing, act, and give concerts for the rest of his life.

Elvis got married in 1967. He and his wife, Priscilla, had a baby in 1968 and named her Lisa Marie. In 1973, Elvis and Priscilla got divorced, and he never married again. Elvis died of heart failure on August 16, 1977.

_____1935_____	Elvis was born in Mississippi.
_____	He got a job with RCA.
_____1967_____	_____
_____1973_____	_____
_____1977_____	_____

Word Study

You already know many of the words on each vocabulary page in the dictionary. As you study, highlight the words that are new for you with a yellow marker. Those are the words that you need to study.

Face and Hair

A Read the description of each woman. Write the letter of the correct picture.

a.   b.   c.

1. This woman has long blond hair. It's straight, about shoulder-length. She has long bangs. She has a friendly face. _____

2. This woman has long blond hair. Her hair is very thick and curly. She usually has braids. She has a pretty face. _____

3. This woman has long blond hair. It's straight. She doesn't have bangs. _____

B Write two or three sentences describing each person.

_____

_____

_____

_____

_____

_____

_____

_____

_____

Write the letter of the correct picture(s) next to each sentence.

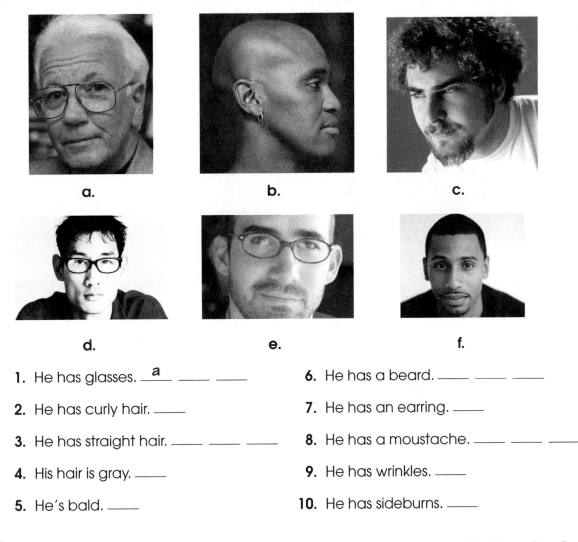

a.

b.

c.

d.

e.

f.

1. He has glasses. __a__ ____ ____

2. He has curly hair. ____

3. He has straight hair. ____ ____ ____

4. His hair is gray. ____

5. He's bald. ____

6. He has a beard. ____ ____ ____

7. He has an earring. ____

8. He has a moustache. ____ ____ ____

9. He has wrinkles. ____

10. He has sideburns. ____

D **Listen to each description. Write the letter of the correct man in Exercise C.**

CD 1
Track 17

1. __c__   2. ____   3. ____   4. ____   5. ____

Word Work **Small Group**

Write the names of the students in your group.

Complete the information about each student.

Name of Student	Hair Color	Hair Length	Hair Style
_____	_____	_____	_____
_____	_____	_____	_____
_____	_____	_____	_____
_____	_____	_____	_____

Daily Activities

A Look in your dictionary. Write the name of the daily activity for each item.

1. _take a coffee break_ 2. _____ 3. _____

4. _____ 5. _____ 6. _____

B Read each sentence. Check *Likely* or *Unlikely*.

	Likely	Unlikely
1. I go to sleep after I get dressed.	____	✓
2. I put on my makeup before I take a shower.	____	____
3. I take a nap after I get up.	____	____
4. I brush my teeth after I eat.	____	____
5. I take a shower after I take a bath.	____	____
6. I take my children to school after we eat dinner.	____	____
7. I watch TV before I go to bed.	____	____
8. I take a walk before I get up.	____	____
9. I get dressed before I take a shower.	____	____
10. I take a walk after I get home from work.	____	____

c Read the information about Marisa and Elena. Find and write about five differences in their schedules.

Marisa

I'm a security guard at an airport. I get up at 6:00 in the morning and eat breakfast. I put on my uniform and go to work. I have a coffee break at 10:00 and I eat lunch at 12:00. Work is over at 3:00. I go to the gym and work out for an hour. I take a shower at the gym. Then, I go home, make dinner, and eat. Two days a week, I go to school. After school, I watch TV for an hour. I go to bed at 11:00.

Elena

I'm a security guard at an airport. I get up at 6:00 in the morning and take a shower. I put on my uniform and go to work. I have a coffee break at 10:30 and I eat lunch at 12:00. Work is over at 3:00. I go home and take a walk for an hour. Then I make dinner and eat. Three days a week, I go to school. After school, I watch TV for an hour. I go to bed at 11:00.

1. ___Marisa eats breakfast in the morning, but Elena doesn't.___

2. _____

3. _____

4. _____

5. _____

D Listen to Eric talk about his schedule. Put his day in order from 1 to 10.

CD 1
Track 18

____ do homework

____ go to gym and work out

____ go to work

____ watch TV

____ get dressed for work

__1__ get up

____ eat dinner

____ eat breakfast

____ take a shower

____ go to bed

Word Work **Partners**

Describe your schedules to one another. Then, write three things that are the same about your schedules. Write three things that are different about your schedules.

Examples: **We both get up at 6:30 in the morning.**

My partner eats breakfast, but I don't.

If you are working alone, write a short paragraph describing your schedule.

Walk, Jump, Run

A   **Look at the picture in your dictionary. Match the question and answer.**

_g_   **1.** Who's getting on the bus?

_____ **2.** Who's going up the stairs?

_____ **3.** Who's leaving the building?

_____ **4.** Who's sitting down?

_____ **5.** Who's running?

_____ **6.** Who's getting off the bus?

_____ **7.** Who's getting out of the taxi?

   a. the boy in the yellow shirt

   b. the woman in the white coat

   c. the boy in the red jacket

   d. the woman in the blue coat

   e. the man in the green jacket

   f. the man in the orange jacket

   g. the woman with the red backpack

B   **Circle the words that can follow each action.**

1. Walk:	(down the stairs)	over a chair	(across the street)
2. Ride:	a bicycle	a chair	a motorcycle
3. Slip:	on the taxi	on the ice	on the banana peel
4. Leave:	the meeting	the classroom	the street
5. Get off:	the taxi	the train	the bus
6. Enter:	the building	the classroom	the bicycle
7. Get out of:	a car	the stairs	a taxi
8. Follow:	the building	the signs	the car

C   **Write the opposite of each sentence.**

1. He's getting on the bus.   _He's getting off the bus._

2. She's going up the stairs.   _____

3. He's entering the building.   _____

4. She's getting into the taxi.   _____

5. He's pushing the wagon.   _____

6. She's sitting down.   _____

D In your notebook, write about the picture. What is each child doing?

Example: Tammy is entering the school building.

Yang   Gloria   Ali   Tammy   Tony   Emily   David   Jenny   Raj

CD 1
Track 19

E Listen and complete the sentences.

1. I _____ leave _____ my apartment at 7:30.

2. I'm always late, so I _____ to the bus stop.

3. I _____ the bus at 14th Street.

4. The bus is always crowded in the morning, so I have to _____.

5. I _____ the bus at 53rd Street.

6. I _____ the street and _____ the building.

7. I _____ the stairs to the third floor.

8. I _____ into my classroom. I _____ and take out my books.

Word Work	Pairs

Explain how you get to school. Be very specific. Write five or more sentences.

1. _____ I leave my . . . _____

2. _____

3. _____

4. _____

5. _____

Feelings

A **Match the definition and the feeling.**

__d__ **1.** worried about a future event   **a.** lonely

____ **2.** peaceful; relaxed   **b.** angry

____ **3.** alone and feeling sad   **c.** full

____ **4.** containing a large amount   **d.** nervous

____ **5.** mad or upset   **e.** bored

____ **6.** feeling sad when you are away from home   **f.** calm

____ **7.** not interested   **g.** homesick

B **Use the chart. Write six sentences.**

He's embarrassed		his father is in the hospital.
He's worried		he just ate two hamburgers.
He's proud	because	he's going on vacation tomorrow.
He's full		he broke your glass.
He's lonely		his son just graduated from college.
He's excited		he has no family in this country.

1. _He's embarrassed because he broke your glass._

2. _____

3. _____

4. _____

5. _____

6. _____

C **Look at the Word Partnerships box on page 39 of the dictionary. Complete the sentences with the correct preposition: *about, of, by.***

1. I'm proud ____*of*____ of my son. He just got his first job.

2. Are you afraid _____ dogs?

3. I'm confused _____ the directions.

4. She's angry _____ the accident. Someone ran a stop sign and hit her car.

5. He's happy _____ his work schedule. He doesn't have to work on

Saturdays.

6. She's tired _____ her long drive to work.

CD 1
Track 20

D **Listen to each situation. How does each person feel?**

1. _____ nervous _____

2. _____

3. _____

4. _____

5. _____

6. _____

> excited
> lonely
> thirsty
> frustrated
> ~~nervous~~
> tired

Word Work **Small Group**

Look at each situation. In your notebook, write about each picture. How does each
person feel? Why? Use *because* in your sentences.

1.

2.

3.

4.

5.

6.

Wave, Greet, Smile

A Write about each picture. What is each person doing?

1.

2.

3.

4.

5.

6.

1. _He is waving good-bye to his family._ _____

2. _____

3. _____

4. _____

5. _____

6. _____

B Complete the sentences with *to* or *with*.

1. I don't agree _____ with _____ you.

2. In some countries, people sometimes bow _____ each other.

3. We shook hands _____ the new employee.

4. He often argues _____ his brother about politics.

5. He danced _____ his girlfriend all night.

6. She waved _____ her neighbor.

7. She apologized _____ the boss for arriving late.

C   Match.

__f__ **1.** When a friend finds a new job,   **a.** you shake hands with her.

____ **2.** When you meet someone new,   **b.** you apologize to her.

____ **3.** When a friend is sad,   **c.** you visit her.

____ **4.** When a friend is in the hospital,   **d.** you comfort her.

____ **5.** When a friend is moving,   **e.** you invite your friends.

____ **6.** When you hurt a friend's feelings,   **f.** you congratulate her.

____ **7.** When a friend gets a new haircut,   **g.** you help her.

____ **8.** When you decide to have a party,   **h.** you compliment her.

CD 1
Track 21

D   Listen to each statement. Write the number of the correct statement next to each action.

____ **a.** He's inviting a friend to his party.

____ **b.** He's introducing two people.

____ **c.** He's agreeing with a friend.

____ **d.** He's greeting a friend.

____ **e.** He's calling a friend.

____ **f.** He's apologizing.

__1__ **g.** He's complimenting a friend.

| **Word Work** | **Partners** |

Agree or disagree with these statements. Give a reason.

1. The driving age should be 18 years old.

2. Drivers should not use cell phones.

3. People should stop driving at 80 years old.

4. All drivers and passengers should wear seat belts.

Documents

A What information does a driver's license contain?

first name _____

_____

_____

DMV **CALIFORNIA** DMV
DRIVER LICENSE
N894...
EXPIRES: 11-13-07
CLASS: C
Susan Hong
452 Austin Street
San Jose, CA 95112
SEX: (F)   HAIR: BLK   EYES: BRN
HT: 5/01   WT: 98   DOB: 01-05-64
Susan Hong
xxxxx   xxx   xx   xxxx

_____

_____

_____

_____

B Name two documents that each person needs or will receive.

a student ID _____

_____

_____

_____

_____

_____

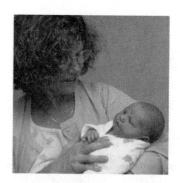

_____

_____

C Complete each sentence with the name of the correct form.

1. You need a _____passport_____ to travel to Japan.

2. You need a _____ to become a teacher.

3. You need a _____ in order to apply to work.

4. A police officer will ask for your _____ and _____ if he stops you for speeding.

5. You have to apply for a _____ in order to live in another country.

6. When you finish high school, you receive a _____.

7. The first week of school, all students receive a _____.

8. Most salespeople give their _____ to customers.

9. You receive a _____ after your wedding.

10. A _____ allows a person from another country to live and work permanently in the United States.

11. An immigrant who becomes a United States citizen receives a _____.

D Write the number of each question next to the correct answer.

CD 1
Track 22

____ **a.** Florida

____ **b.** Menendez

____ **c.** 4 / 21 / 85

____ **d.** 15467190

____ **e.** cpg22@bluebird.com

____ **f.** Miami

____ **g.** 555-9847

_1_ **h.** 33142

____ **i.** P.

____ **j.** Carlos

Word Work Partners

Take out two documents you have in your wallet or purse.
Discuss or list the information that each form contains.

Nationalities

A **Write three nationalities that end with these letters.**

- an	- ese	- ish
Nigerian		

B **Write the nationality.**

1. Canada   Canadian
2. Germany
3. Chile
4. Turkey
5. Thailand
6. Japan

7. Vietnam
8. Brazil
9. Argentina
10. Philippines
11. Australia
12. United States

C **Guess the nationality of these famous people. (Check your answers at the bottom of page 45.)**

Italian	Chinese	~~Spanish~~	Russian	Brazilian
French	British	American	Indian	Greek

1. Pablo Picasso was a famous _____Spanish_____ artist.
2. Shakespeare was a famous _____ writer.
3. Yuri Gagarin was a famous _____ astronaut.
4. Pele is a famous _____ soccer player.
5. Gustave Eiffel was a famous _____ architect.
6. Thomas Edison was a famous _____ inventor.
7. Mohandas Ghandi was a famous _____ leader.
8. Aristotle was a famous _____ philosopher.
9. Confucius was a famous _____ thinker.
10. Michelangelo was a famous _____ artist.

D **Listen and complete each sentence with the nationality you hear.**

CD 1
Track 23

1. Hot dogs are a favorite _____American_____ food.

2. A _____ croissant is delicious.

3. You can enjoy delicious _____ pasta in many restaurants.

4. _____ caviar is the best in the world.

5. You can order paella at the _____ restaurant in town.

6. _____ coffee is rich and flavorful.

7. Baklava is a sweet _____ dessert.

8. The new _____ restaurant has wonderful sushi.

9. Some _____ curries are mild, but others are very hot.

10. That store sells delicious _____ empanadas.

Word Work **Class**

Write the names of five students in your class. Write the name of each person's country and nationality.

Name	Country	Nationality
_____	_____	_____
_____	_____	_____
_____	_____	_____
_____	_____	_____
_____	_____	_____

Word Study

Write a few of your new words on an index card. Put the card in your pocket or purse. Take out the card several times a day to study the words.

Exercise C: 1. Spanish 2. British 3. Russian 4. Brazilian 5. French 6. American 7. Indian 8. Greek 9. Chinese 10. Italian

45

Places Around Town

A **Look in your dictionary. Complete the sentences.**

1. The library is next to the _____courthouse_____.

2. The _____ is between the school and the motel.

3. The fire station is across from the _____.

4. The _____ is behind the college.

5. The _____ is between the stadium and the school.

6. The parking garage is next to the _____.

7. The _____ is in front of the college.

8. The _____ is in front of the church.

B **Write six sentences using some of these cues. Give the name of the place.**

buy stamps	~~see a movie~~	park my car
get some gas	pay my parking ticket	get a dog license
apply for a job	look for a good book	watch a baseball game

1. _____I'm going to see a movie at the movie theater._____

2. _____

3. _____

4. _____

5. _____

6. _____

C **Write the place you can associate with these words.**

1. judge, jury, lawyer   _____a courthouse_____

2. doctor, operation, patient   _____

3. stamp, letter, mailbox   _____

4. student, teacher, test   _____

5. room, bed, reservation   _____

6. screen, seat, tickets _____

7. parking lot, stores, shopping bag _____

D **Match the statement and the place.**

_d_ **1.** How much is this red convertible?   **a.** college

_____ **2.** We have a report of a fire on Oak Road.   **b.** post office

_____ **3.** I'd like to send this package.   **c.** police station

_____ **4.** The baseball score is now 5–3.   **d.** car dealership

_____ **5.** Your final exam is next Monday.   **e.** city hall

_____ **6.** I need a copy of my birth certificate.   **f.** stadium

_____ **7.** You're under arrest for stealing a car.   **g.** fire station

E **Listen to each statement and write the letter of the correct place.**

CD 1
Track 24

a.   b.   c.

1. _b_   **2.** ___   **3.** ___   **4.** ___   **5.** ___

6. ___   **7.** ___   **8.** ___   **9.** ___

Word Work   **Small Group**

Complete the sentences. Discuss your answers with your group.

1. I would like to live next to a _____.

2. I would not like to live next to a _____.

3. I'd like to work at a _____.

4. A small town usually doesn't have a _____.

5. When I have time, I enjoy going to a _____.

Shops and Stores

A Write the kind of store where you can buy these items.

1. <u>a clothing store</u> : coat   shirt   dress

2. _____ : table   chair   sofa

3. _____ : aspirin   toothpaste   prescription

4. _____ : calendar   book   magazine

5. _____ : ring   watch   necklace

6. _____ : cat   dog   fish

7. _____ : stereo   television   computer

B Complete the sentences.

1. You can exercise at a <u>health club</u>.

2. You can wash your clothes at a _____.

3. You can rent a movie at a _____.

4. You can order a birthday cake at a _____.

5. You can order a cappuccino or espresso at a _____.

6. You can get a haircut at a _____.

7. You can get a manicure at a _____.

8. You can make a copy of a document at a _____.

9. You can pick up your clean suit at a _____.

10. You can order a hamburger and french fries at a _____.

CD 1
Track 25

C Listen to a woman talk about her trip to the mall. She went to eight
different stores. Where did she go first, second, third, etc.? Put the correct
number in front of each store.

_____ Toy store   <u>1</u> Beauty salon

_____ Jewelry store   _____ Pet store

_____ Bakery   _____ Flea market

_____ Bookstore   _____ Clothing store

D Write a sentence about each picture. Use the name of a store in the sentence.

1. 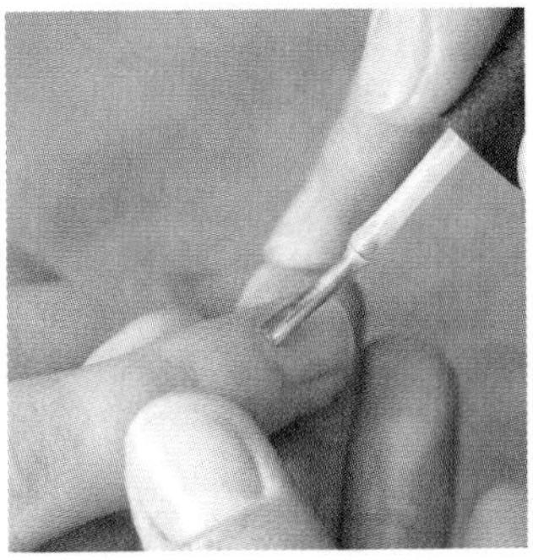
2. 
3.

4. 
5. 
6.

1. _She is getting a manicure at a nail salon._

2. _____

3. _____

4. _____

5. _____

6. _____

Word Work Small Group

Many stores are chain stores that sell the same items in all their locations. Name three well-known stores in each category. Talk about which stores you like.

Supermarkets: _____ _____ _____

Clothing stores: _____ _____ _____

Coffee shops: _____ _____ _____

Drugstores: _____ _____ _____

Bank

A **Look in your dictionary. Complete the definitions.**

1. A _____loan officer_____ is a person who helps customers apply for loans.

2. A _____ is a person who keeps money in a bank.

3. A _____ is a person who watches customers carefully.

4. A _____ is a person who manages the work in a bank.

5. A _____ is a person who works at the teller window.

B **Read the dialogues below. Write the correct response from the box.**

> Your check is going to bounce.
> Endorse the back of the check and fill out a deposit slip.
> ~~Your balance is $850.~~
> Fill out a withdrawal slip.
> They're in the vault.
> Talk with the loan officer.

1. **a:** How much money is in my checking account?

   b: _____Your balance is $850._____

2. **a:** I'd like to buy a car, but I don't have enough money.

   b: _____

3. **a:** I'd like to deposit my paycheck.

   b: _____

4. **a:** I'd like to take some money out of my account.

   b: _____

5. **a:** I wrote a check for $500, but I only have $200 in my checking account.

   b: _____

6. **a:** Where are the safe-deposit boxes?

   b: _____

C **Match.**

_e_ **1.** He took money out of the bank.   **a.** His balance is $600.

___ **2.** He put money in the bank.   **b.** He endorsed his check.

___ **3.** He signed the back of his check.   **c.** He inserted his ATM card.

___ **4.** He has $600 in the bank.   **d.** He deposited money.

___ **5.** He put his card in the ATM.   **e.** He withdrew money.

___ **6.** He took his card from the ATM.   **f.** He removed his ATM card.

CD 1
Track 26

D **Listen to the information about World Bank and City Bank. Which offers better service?**

	World Bank	City Bank
ATMs	_____	_____
Tellers	_____	_____
Interest on savings	_____	_____
Drive-up windows	_____	_____
Safe-deposit boxes	_____	_____

Word Work **Pairs**

Read the sentences and fill out the savings account passbook. Use your imagination and show two more transactions.

1. On May 4th, Ahmed opened a savings account. He made a deposit of $1,300.

2. On May 15th, Ahmed made a deposit of $400.

3. On May 23rd, Ahmed made a deposit of $200.

4. On May 30th, Ahmed received $2.35 in interest.

5. On June 6th, Ahmed made a withdrawal of $500.

6. On June 18th, Ahmed made a deposit of $800.

SAVINGS ACCOUNT

DATE	NOTE	% INTEREST	+DEPOSITS	– WITHDRAWALS	BALANCE
5/4	deposit		1,300.00		1,300.00

Post Office

A **Look at the picture in your dictionary. Circle *T* if the statement is true. Circle *F* if the statement is false.**

1. A woman is sending a letter by overnight delivery. (T) F

2. There's a package on the counter. T F

3. A postal clerk is weighing a package. T F

4. Someone is buying stamps at the stamp machine. T F

5. A mail truck is in front of the post office. T F

6. Someone is putting a letter in the mailbox. T F

7. A woman is looking in her post office box. T F

B **Write the correct response after each question or statement.**

Yes, there's one on the corner.	I sent it by overnight mail.
He comes about noon.	Send me a postcard.
~~Use the stamp machine.~~	Put it on the scale.
Did you send her a greeting card?	07024

1. I need some stamps. _____Use the stamp machine._____

2. What's your zip code? _____

3. It's my sister's birthday. _____

4. Is there a mailbox near here? _____

5. How much does this package weigh? _____

6. When does your mail carrier come? _____

7. I'm going on vacation next week. _____

8. How did you send the package? _____

Complete the sentences.

| postage-paid | sheet | love letter | ~~roll~~ |
| postmark | bill | greeting cards | |

1. A _____roll_____ of stamps has one hundred stamps.

2. A _____ of stamps has twenty stamps.

3. The telephone company sends me a _____ every month.

4. Many people send _____ to their friends on their birthdays.

5. You don't need to put a stamp on a _____ envelope.

6. Did you ever receive a _____ from your boyfriend/girlfriend?

7. The _____ shows the postage and the date sent.

D **Listen to the conversations. Write the word or phrase you hear.**

CD 1
Track 27

1. _____*sheet of stamps*_____

2. _____

3. _____

4. _____

5. _____

6. _____

7. _____

| package |
| postcard |
| ~~sheet of stamps~~ |
| mailbox |
| mail carrier |
| zip code |
| overnight mail |

Word Work **Pairs**

Tell your group about each piece of mail you received yesterday.

What did you do with each piece?

What mail did you receive?

- a bill
- a letter
- a postcard
- overnight mail
- a package
- a catalog
- a greeting card

What did you do with it?

1. I opened it.
2. I looked at the _____.
3. I read it.
4. I paid the _____.
5. I threw it away.

Library

A Look at the library in your dictionary. Complete these word partnerships.

1. library _____*card*_____

2. circulation _____

3. online _____

4. paperback _____

5. reference _____

6. microfilm _____

B Circle *T* if the statement is true. Circle *F* if the statement is false.

1. You need a library card to check out a book.   Ⓣ   F

2. The headline in a newspaper gives the daily weather.   T   F

3. The cover of a book tells the title and the author.   T   F

4. You check out a book at the reference desk.   T   F

5. The librarian can help you find a book.   T   F

6. Look in the online catalog to find the location of a book in the library.   T   F

7. Young children enjoy looking at picture books.   T   F

8. The reading room is a quiet area in the library.   T   F

9. A novel is the story of a famous person's life.   T   F

C Put these steps in order.

_____ Ana wrote the number and location of the books on a piece of paper.

_____ She checked out two books.

__1__ Ana went to the library to find a book about digital photography.

_____ She returned the books to the library.

_____ She used the numbers to find the books in the nonfiction section.

_____ She went to the circulation desk.

_____ She took the books home and read them.

_____ She used the online catalog to find books on digital photography.

D Circle two items you can find in each section of the library.

1. periodical section: (a newspaper) (a magazine) a biography
2. fiction section: a romance novel a dictionary a detective novel
3. reference section: a novel an atlas an encyclopedia
4. nonfiction section: a cookbook a novel an autobiography

CD 1
Track 28

E Where can each person look for the information he/she needs? Listen and write the number of each sentence under the correct picture.

What's for Dessert?

WORLD ATLAS

World News
One of America's Finest Daily Newspapers

ALL SURVIVE LANDING
OF SMALL JET AS PILOT
MISSES RUNWAY
AT NEARBY AIRPORT

a. _____ b. _____ c. _____

World Encyclopedia
W

Finance Weekly

May 23

English Dictionary

d. _____ e. ____1____ f. _____

Word Work Small Group

Ask your group members about the library in your area.

Name: _____ _____ _____

1. Do you have a library card? _____ _____ _____
2. How often do you go to the library? _____ _____ _____
3. What kinds of books do you like to read? _____ _____ _____
4. What newspaper do you read? _____ _____ _____
5. What is your favorite magazine? _____ _____ _____

Daycare Center

A Look at the daycare center in your dictionary. Answer the questions.

a newborn	a baby	a toddler	a preschooler

1. Who is in the high chair? _____a toddler_____

2. Who is on the rest mat? _____

3. Who is playing with toys on the floor? _____

4. Who is in the baby carrier? _____

5. Who is in the stroller? _____

6. Who is on the changing table? _____

B Check the correct age. It is possible to check two or more answers.

	Newborn	Baby	Toddler	Preschooler
1. puts away toys	___	___	✓	✓
2. sleeps in a crib	___	___	___	___
3. wears diapers	___	___	___	___
4. wears training pants	___	___	___	___
5. drinks formula	___	___	___	___
6. can use a potty chair	___	___	___	___
7. sits in a high chair	___	___	___	___

C Complete the definitions.

1. A bed for a baby: _____a crib_____

2. A person who works in a daycare center: _____

3. The top part of a baby's bottle: _____

4. A toy that a baby shakes and it makes a noise: _____

5. A liquid food for babies: _____

6. A small compartment for coats and bags: _____

D Check the correct response: *Good idea* or *Bad idea*.

	Good idea	Bad idea
1. Put dirty diapers in a diaper pail.	✓	
2. Put training pants on a newborn.		
3. Put formula in a bottle.		
4. Put a bib on a toddler.		
5. Give a preschooler a bottle.		
6. Use diaper pins with a disposable diaper.		
7. Put a preschooler in a baby carrier.		
8. Show a preschooler how to share toys.		

CD 1
Track 29

E Listen to this mother's schedule. Then, answer the questions.

1. What does this mother do as soon as the baby wakes up?

   She changes his diaper.

2. What does she give him after she changes his diaper?

   _____

3. Where does she put him after breakfast?

   _____

4. What does the baby do while she packs his bag?

   _____

5. What does she pack for the daycare center?

   _____

6. What doesn't she pack?

   _____

Word Work **Pairs**

You are leaving your one-year-old baby with a babysitter for the evening. Write a list of instructions that you need to give the babysitter.

   Example: *Give the baby a bottle at 6:00 and again at 10:00.*

City Square

A Look at the picture in your dictionary. Circle *T* if the statement is true. Circle *F* if the statement is false.

1.	Two drivers had a traffic accident.	Ⓣ	F
2.	The accident happened in front of the bank.	T	F
3.	A cop is directing traffic around the accident.	T	F
4.	The handicapped parking space is empty.	T	F
5.	Four pedestrians are in the crosswalk.	T	F
6.	Two people are standing at the tourist information booth.	T	F
7.	The street musician is playing a violin.	T	F
8.	There is a statue of a man on a horse in front of the art museum.	T	F
9.	The travel information booth is in front of the science museum.	T	F
10.	The fire hydrant is next to the monument.	T	F

B Look in your dictionary. How many people do you see . . .

1. in front of the art gallery? __2__

2. in the crosswalk? ____

3. sitting in front of the café? ____

4. at the street vendor? ____

5. at the newsstand? ____

6. at the tourist information booth? ____

7. looking at the traffic accident? ____

8. walking into the museum? ____

C Complete the traffic and safety rules.

1. Do not park in front of a ____fire hydrant____.

2. Put money in the _____.

3. Call the police if you have a _____.

4. Cars must stop for pedestrians in the _____.

5. You need a special license to park in a _____.

6. Do not throw anything on the _____.

> parking meter
> sidewalk
> handicapped parking space
> ~~fire hydrant~~
> crosswalk
> traffic accident

D **Match the questions and answers.**

_c_ 1. Why did you get a ticket?

_____ 2. Can I park here?

_____ 3. What does the billboard say?

_____ 4. Where is the newsstand?

_____ 5. Why did the driver call the cops?

_____ 6. Where can I get a map of the city?

_____ 7. Do you have money for the parking meter?

a. Keep Our City Clean!

b. Try the tourist information booth.

c. I parked in front of a hydrant.

d. He had an accident.

e. Parking is free on Sunday.

f. It's in front of the art museum.

g. No, it's a handicapped parking space.

E **A tourist just arrived in this city. Listen and number the places he went in the correct order.**

CD 1
Track 30

_____ the tourist information booth

_____ the café

_____ the art museum

_____ the bank

_1_ the hotel

_____ the travel agency

Word Work **Small Group**

How is this street scene in the dictionary the same as the street in front of your school?

Example: **There's a bank across the street from our school.**

_____

_____

How is this street scene different from the street in front of your school?

Example: **There isn't a museum on this street.**

_____

_____

Crime and Justice

A **Look in your dictionary. Complete the definitions.**

1. Starting a fire in a building: _____ *arson* _____

2. Stealing a car: _____

3. Stealing items from a store: _____

4. Destroying property: _____

5. Selling illegal drugs: _____

6. Illegally paying money in return for favors: _____

7. Killing a person: _____

8. Entering a house or building and stealing items: _____

B **Match the headline and the crime.**

_d_ **1.** Boy Arrested for Spray Painting Church   **a.** mugging

____ **2.** Actress Charged with Taking Fur Coat from Store   **b.** murder

____ **3.** Man Arrested for Killing His Brother   **c.** auto theft

____ **4.** Video Shows Man with Gun Running from Bank   **d.** graffiti

____ **5.** Police Stop Street Fight   **e.** shoplifting

____ **6.** Woman Hurt as Man Grabs Pocketbook   **f.** armed robbery

____ **7.** Ten Residents Report Cars Stolen   **g.** gang violence

C **Read and circle the correct words.**

Last year, Maya was the (victim   criminal) of a crime. A man with a knife

mugged her. A (witness   judge) saw the mugging and called the (police

lawyer). The police made (an arrest   a trial) the same day. The next month, there

was a (trial   theft) in a (prison   courtroom). The (police   jury) listened to the

(lawyers   murder). They decided that the man was guilty. The (judge   witness)

sent the man to (courtroom   prison) for one year.

60

D Complete the sentences with *robbed* or *stole*.

1. A man _____robbed_____ the bank.

2. He _____ $2,000.

3. Someone _____ my house.

4. He _____ my computer.

5. Someone _____ my car.

6. Someone _____ the gift shop.

steal – stole
A person <u>steals</u> a thing.
She <u>stole</u> $50.
She <u>stole</u> my camera.
rob – robbed
A person <u>robs</u> a place.
She <u>robbed</u> the bank.
She <u>robbed</u> the jewelry store.

CD 1
Track 31

E Listen to the description of each crime. Circle the letter of the crime.

1. **(a.)** burglary   **b.** vandalism   **c.** bribery

2. **a.** drunk driving   **b.** bribery   **c.** auto theft

3. **a.** burglary   **b.** vandalism   **c.** arson

4. **a.** mugging   **b.** drunk driving   **c.** drug dealing

5. **a.** arson   **b.** theft   **c.** graffiti

6. **a.** auto theft   **b.** drunk driving   **c.** mugging

Word Work | **Small Group**

You are the jury. What sentence will you give for each crime?

Crime	Sentence
1. Shoplifting a pair of jeans	_____
2. Stealing a car	_____
3. Murdering a person	_____
4. Robbing a store with a gun	_____

Word Study

You will often see one of your new words in a newspaper, in a store, or on a sign. If it's a word that you are learning, copy down the sentence or phrase.

Examples: **The jury found the man guilty of <u>armed robbery</u>. (pp. 60–61)**
                    <u>Drive-up</u> Banking <u>Window</u> (pp. 50–51)

Types of Homes

A Where might each person live? Write a different type of home for each picture.

1. 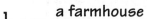 a farmhouse

2. _____

3. _____

4. _____

5. _____

6. _____

B Write two types of homes you often find in each location. You may use the same type of home more than once.

The City	The Suburbs
a condominium	_____
_____	_____

A Small Town	The Country
_____	_____
_____	_____

Complete the sentences with a type of home.

1. ___A houseboat___ is on the water.

2. _____ is a house of snow.

3. A family who lives on _____ has horses.

4. One family lives on one side of _____ and another family lives on the other side.

5. Students often live in _____ .

6. People who live in _____ can move their home.

7. A family who lives in _____ usually grows corn, tomatoes, or other vegetables.

8. There are many _____ in that building. The tenants pay rent.

9. The British royal family lives in a large _____ in London.

CD 1
Track 32

D **Listen to each speaker. Write the number of each statement next to the correct type of home.**

____ **a.** houseboat   ____ **e.** apartment

__1__ **b.** townhouse   ____ **f.** dormitory

____ **c.** mobile home   ____ **g.** farmhouse

____ **d.** house   ____ **h.** retirement home

Word Work **Small Group**

Choose two types of homes. Write one advantage to each type of home. Write one disadvantage.

Type of home: _____

Advantage: _____

Disadvantage: _____

Type of home: _____

Advantage: _____

Disadvantage: _____

Finding a Place to Live

A Which type of housing does each statement refer to?
Check *Apartment, House,* or *Both.*

	Apartment	House	Both
1. Meet the landlord.	✓	___	___
2. Call a realtor.	___	___	___
3. Ask questions.	___	___	___
4. Apply for a loan.	___	___	___
5. Sign a lease.	___	___	___
6. Make a down payment.	___	___	___
7. Get the key.	___	___	___
8. Meet the neighbors.	___	___	___
9. Pay the rent.	___	___	___

B Complete the sentences about renting an apartment.

1. Many people _____ **look for** _____ an apartment in the classified ads in the

   newspaper.

2. In order to see the apartment, you have to _____.

3. When you see the apartment, you should _____.

4. At the time you sign the lease, you must also _____.

5. Every month, a tenant has to _____.

C Complete the sentences about buying a house with *before* or *after.*

1. You look at houses _____ **after** _____ you call a realtor.

2. You look at several houses _____ you make a decision.

3. You make an offer _____ you decide on a house.

4. You inspect the house _____ you move in.

5. You begin to make the house payments _____ you move in.

D **Wu and Ling bought a house last year. Read the paragraph and write the correct amounts below.**

Wu and Ling Cho called a realtor last year and began looking at houses. They looked at about twenty homes and finally found one they liked. The price was $240,000. Wu and Ling made an offer of $220,000. The realtors negotiated the price, and the two families agreed on a price of $230,000. Wu and Ling made a down payment of $25,000, and they applied for a loan of $205,000 from a local bank. Two months later, Wu and Ling moved into their new home. Each month, they make a payment of $1,300.

The asking price of the house was ___$240,000___.

The Chos made an offer of _____.

The realtors negotiated a price of _____.

The Chos made a down payment of _____.

The Chos applied for a loan for _____.

They make a house payment of _____ a month.

CD 1
Track 33

E **Listen to Louis's story about renting an apartment. Put the sentences in order from 1 to 8.**

_____ He paid a security deposit.

_____ He is going to pack.

_____ The landlord is going to give him the key.

__1__ He looked for an apartment.

_____ They're going to unpack.

_____ He signed the lease.

_____ They're going to arrange the furniture.

_____ They're going to load the van.

Word Work	Small Group

Write three questions you should ask the landlord when you look at an apartment.

1. _____

2. _____

3. _____

Apartment Building

A Look at the apartment building in your dictionary. Match the location of each person, place, or thing.

_f_ **1.** The doorman is   **a.** in the center of the building.

___ **2.** The workout room is   **b.** in back of the building.

___ **3.** The courtyard is   **c.** in the door.

___ **4.** The storage area is   **d.** on the second floor.

___ **5.** The air conditioner is   **e.** in the basement.

___ **6.** The laundry room is   **f.** in front of the building.

___ **7.** The peephole is   **g.** in the window.

B Complete the apartment building rules.

doorman	parking space	dead-bolt
super	~~intercom~~	air conditioner
hallway	peephole	dumpster

1. Use the ___**intercom**___ before you let someone into the building.

2. Be safe. Always lock your door with the _____.

3. If someone knocks on your door, look through the _____ before you open the door.

4. If you are expecting a package, speak with the _____ as you leave the building.

5. Save electricity. Turn off your _____ when you leave your apartment.

6. Each apartment has one _____. Visitors must park on the street.

7. Do not leave boxes or trash in the _____. Put all trash in the _____ in back of the building.

8. Report any problems to the _____.

C Read the questions. Then, write the correct answer from the box.

> There's a workout room.
> The dumpster is on the side of the building.
> Yes. And there's a door chain, too.
> Call the super.
> ~~Each apartment has one parking space.~~
> There's a laundry room.

1. Is there parking? _____ Each apartment has one parking space. _____

2. Where do I put the trash? _____

3. Where can I do my wash? _____

4. Is there a place to exercise? _____

5. Is there a dead-bolt on the door? _____

6. Who do I call if I have a problem? _____

CD 1
Track 34

D Listen to Sheri speak with her mother about three apartments for rent. Complete the chart as you listen.

	Size	Parking		Distance to work	Rent
1.	small studio	(Yes)	No	_____	_____
2.	_____	Yes	No	_____	_____
3.	_____	Yes	No	_____	_____

E Which apartment do you think that Sheri should rent? Give two reasons.

_____

_____

_____

Word Work Partners

Sit with a partner. Write a conversation between a super and a person looking for an apartment to rent.

House and Garden

A **Look in your dictionary. Match the item and the location.**

  _d_ **1.** The vegetable garden is

_____ **2.** The rake is

_____ **3.** The hammock is

_____ **4.** The trash can is

_____ **5.** The grill is

_____ **6.** The shutters are

_____ **7.** The wheelbarrow is

a. in the garage.

b. on the deck.

c. next to the garage.

d. in front of the fence.

e. on the windows.

f. in the front yard.

g. in the backyard.

B **Complete the sentences.**

1. Close the _____ door _____.

2. Cut the _____.

3. Put the car in the _____.

4. Light the _____.

5. Lie in the _____.

6. Open the _____.

7. Put the trash in the _____.

8. Ring the _____.

9. Water the grass with the _____.

| doorbell |
| grill |
| hammock |
| garbage can |
| grass |
| ~~door~~ |
| hose |
| window |
| garage |

C **Complete the definitions.**

1. _____ A skylight _____ is a window in a roof.

2. _____ tells you that someone is at the door.

3. _____ is a building for a car.

4. _____ is a door in a fence.

5. _____ is a machine used to cut grass.

6. _____ is the space under a roof, often used to store things.

D Write the correct response after each statement.

The lawnmower is broken.   Relax in the hammock.
I just turned on the sprinkler.   ~~I'll heat up the grill.~~
I didn't hear the doorbell.   I'll open the windows.

1. It's time to start dinner.   *I'll heat up the grill.*

2. I'm really tired.   _____

3. It's hot in the house today.   _____

4. Please cut the grass.   _____

5. Please water the grass.   _____

6. Is someone at the door?   _____

CD 1
Track 35

E Look at the picture in the dictionary. Circle the correct answer.

1. **(a.)** Yes, it is.   **b.** No, it isn't.

2. **a.** Yes, it is.   **b.** No, it isn't.

3. **a.** Yes, it is.   **b.** No, it isn't.

4. **a.** Yes, they are.   **b.** No, they aren't.

5. **a.** Yes, it is.   **b.** No, it isn't.

6. **a.** Yes, they are.   **b.** No, they aren't.

7. **a.** Yes, it is.   **b.** No, it isn't.

Word Work **Partners**

In your notebook, write ten sentences about the two houses. Describe the differences.

Example: **House A has a porch, but House B doesn't.**

House A   House B

Kitchen and Dining Area

A Look at the kitchen in your dictionary. Write the location of each item.

1. Would you like a _____ *glass* _____ of water?

2. Please light the _____ on the table.

3. Put the yogurt in the _____ and the ice cream in the
   _____ .

4. Please empty the _____ . The dishes are clean.

5. The dishes are in the _____ above the blender.

6. The pan is very hot! Use the _____ .

7. Put the banana peel in the _____ , not the wastebasket.

8. Turn the _____ to 350°.

9. Dry the dishes with a _____ .

10. The toaster is on the _____ .

B Write the item you use to make the food in each picture.

1. ____*coffeemaker*____   2. _____   3. _____   4. _____

C Cross out the word that does not belong.

1. ~~shelf~~   coffeemaker   toaster   blender

2. mug   placemat   glass   cup

3. oven   stove   freezer   microwave

4. napkin   dishwasher   oven   refrigerator

5. dishes   plate   bowl   toaster

70

D Read each statement. Check *Good idea* or *Bad idea*.

		Good idea	Bad idea
1.	Put the plate in the toaster.	——	✓
2.	Put the dirty dishes in the dishwasher.	——	——
3.	Put the silverware in the microwave.	——	——
4.	Put the bread in the toaster.	——	——
5.	Put the napkins on the table.	——	——
6.	Put the candles in the oven.	——	——
7.	Put the glasses in the garbage disposal.	——	——
8.	Put the milk in the refrigerator.	——	——
9.	Put the kettle on the stove.	——	——

CD 1
Track 36

E Look at the place setting. You will hear eight statements. Write the four statements that are true.

1. _____

2. _____

3. _____

4. _____

Word Work **Partners**

Write or discuss: How is your kitchen similar to the kitchen in the dictionary? How is your kitchen different?

This kitchen has a table and two chairs. My kitchen has a table and four chairs.

This kitchen has a microwave. I don't need a microwave.

Living Room

A Complete the name of each item in the living room.

1. fire _____ *screen* _____
2. smoke _____
3. throw _____
4. curtain _____
5. ceiling _____

6. coffee _____
7. house _____
8. love _____
9. rocking _____
10. wall _____

B Complete the sentences about the picture in the dictionary.

1. The _____ *house plant* _____ looks dry. Please water it.

2. Sit down and put your feet on the _____.

3. Please don't smoke. The _____ will go off.

4. You can sit on the _____ and look out the window.

5. Don't put your feet on the _____.

6. Please put the book in the _____.

7. You can set the temperature in the room with the _____.

8. The television is in the_____.

9. There are two _____ in the living room, one is on the end table

   and one is on the mantel.

C Cross out the word that does not belong.

1.	sofa	~~wall unit~~	cushion	throw pillow
2.	curtain rod	blinds	curtain	ottoman
3.	mantel	wall	fireplace	fire screen
4.	rocking chair	sofa	vent	loveseat
5.	floor	ceiling	wall	armchair
6.	loveseat	light switch	lamp	lampshade

D Match.

_f_ **1.** If you are hot,
     a. turn on a lamp.

_____ **2.** If you are cold,
     b. close the blinds.

_____ **3.** If it's too sunny,
     c. take a nap on the sofa.

_____ **4.** If it's too dark,
     d. start a fire.

_____ **5.** If you are tired,
     e. put the fire screen in front of the fireplace.

_____ **6.** If you want a good book,
     f. turn on the ceiling fan.

_____ **7.** If you start a fire,
     g. look in the bookcase.

CD 1
Track 37

E Look at the picture of the living room and listen to the statements. Circle _T_ if the statement is true. Circle _F_ if the statement is false.

1. T	(F)	6. T	F
2. T	F	7. T	F
3. T	F	8. T	F
4. T	F	9. T	F
5. T	F	10. T	F

Word Work | Partners

The owners of this new home have a living room with a fireplace. So far, they have bought two chairs and an end table for the living room. What five items should they buy next? What colors should they choose for the items?

1. _____

2. _____

3. _____

4. _____

5. _____

Bedroom and Bathroom

A **Look at the picture in your dictionary. Write the location of each item.**

1. The mirror is _____*over the dresser.*_____

2. The lamp is _____

3. The alarm clock is _____

4. The dresser is _____

5. The yellow and black rug is _____

6. The medicine cabinet is _____

7. The wastebasket is _____

8. The plunger is _____

9. The washcloth is _____

B **Complete the sentences.**

1. You close the _____*shower curtain*_____ when you take a shower.

2. You turn on the _____ when you wash your hands.

3. You dry your hands on a _____.

4. You keep aspirin and other medications in the _____.

5. You close the _____ when you go to sleep.

6. You set the _____ to the time you want to get up.

7. You put your head on a _____ when you go to sleep.

8. You hang your clothes in the _____.

9. You look in the _____ when you get dressed.

C **Circle the items that can complete this sentence.**

Please close the _____.

medicine cabinet   towel   drawer

closet   toilet seat   blanket

lamp   shower curtain   shade

D Write the correct answer after each question.

> It's on the night table.   It's a king.
>
> I like two.   No, I have a small rug.
>
> They're blue.   ~~No, it's part of the bathtub.~~

1. Do you have a separate shower?   <u>No, it's part of the bathtub.</u>

2. What size bed do you have?   _____

3. What color are your towels?   _____

4. Where is your alarm clock?   _____

5. Do you have a carpet on the floor?   _____

6. How many pillows do you like?   _____

CD 1
Track 38

E Listen to the speaker. Check if she is describing something that she likes or doesn't like about her bedroom and bathroom.

	She likes it.	She doesn't like it.
1. closet	____	✓
2. bed	____	____
3. mirror	____	____
4. carpet	____	____
5. bathroom	____	____
6. medicine cabinet	____	____

Word Work   **Partners**

Close your dictionaries. How much do you remember about the bathroom in your dictionary? Add all the bathroom items you remember to this picture.

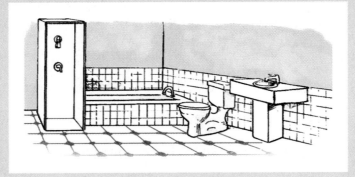

Household Problems

A Which repair person do you associate with each picture?

1. _____meter reader_____   2. _____   3. _____

4. _____   5. _____   6. _____

B Write the person that each homeowner needs to call.

1. The roof leaks.   _____You need to call a roofer._____

2. I want a new light in the kitchen.   _____

3. We need a new lock on the front door.   _____

4. We have cockroaches.   _____

5. The front window is broken.   _____

6. The kitchen faucet drips.   _____

7. I think our gas bill is too high.   _____

C Circle two words you can use with each problem.

1. The ((toilet)   (sink)   roof) is clogged.

2. The (ceiling   lightbulb   roof) leaks.

3. The (window   air conditioner   power) is broken.

4. The (power   pipe   electricity) is out.

5. The (wall   heater   light) doesn't work.

6. The (basement   bathroom   lock) is flooded.

D Read the two problems. If the meaning is the same, write *S*. If the meaning is different, write *D*.

1. **a.** The basement is flooded.   **b.** There is water on the basement floor.   _S_

2. **a.** The power is out.   **b.** We don't have any electricity.   ____

3. **a.** The pipes are frozen.   **b.** The pipes are clogged.   ____

4. **a.** The lock is jammed.   **b.** We can't unlock the door.   ____

5. **a.** The faucet drips.   **b.** We can't turn on the water.   ____

6. **a.** The heater doesn't work.   **b.** We don't have any heat.   ____

7. **a.** The lightbulb is burned out.   **b.** The lightbulb is cracked.   ____

CD 1
Track 39

E Listen and look at the pictures of the bathroom and kitchen. If the sentence is true, circle *T*. If the sentence is false, circle *F*.

1. T (F)   3. T   F   5. T   F   7. T   F

2. T   F   4. T   F   6. T   F   8. T   F

Word Work | **Partners**

Read the problems below. Check the three you think are the most serious.

☐ The lock is jammed.   ☐ The roof leaks.

☐ The power is out.   ☐ The toilet is clogged.

☐ The pipes are frozen.   ☐ The basement is flooded.

☐ The house has termites.   ☐ The house has ants.

Household Chores

A **Look at the picture in the dictionary. What chores do you do?**
Write three chores in each group.

I do this every day:	I do this once a week:	I never do this:
_____	_____	_____
_____	_____	_____
_____	_____	_____

B **Complete the sentences.**

1. The wastebasket is full.   Please ___*empty*___ it.

2. The dishes are dirty.   Please _____ them.

3. The dirty laundry is in the basket.   Please _____ it.

4. The bills are on the desk.   Please _____ them.

5. The dishes are wet.   Please _____ them.

6. The clean clothes are in the dryer.   Please _____ them.

7. The grass is tall.   Please _____ it.

8. The lawn is dry.   Please _____ it.

dry
wash
pay
wash
fold
mow
~~empty~~
water

C **Circle the two words that can follow each action.**

1. wash: (the car)   (the dishes)   the trash

2. put away: the clothes   the sink   the dishes

3. fold: the wastebasket   the clothes   the sheets

4. do: the laundry   the dishes   the rug

5. clean: the sink   the bills   the kitchen

6. polish: the rug   the furniture   the car

7. make: the dinner   the leaves   the bed

D This college student needs to clean his dorm room. On a piece of paper, explain what he needs to do.

Example: **There is a lot of paper in his wastebasket. He needs to empty it.**

CD 1
Track 40

E It's Saturday, and Lidia and Luis cleaned today. Look at each person's To Do List. Listen to the speaker and check the chores they completed.

Lidia - To Do
- ☑ clean the bedroom
- ☐ change the sheets
- ☐ do the laundry
- ☐ clean the bathroom
- ☐ scrub the toilet
- ☐ clean the sink
- ☐ mop the floor
- ☐ clean the kitchen
- ☐ cook dinner

Luis - To Do
- ☐ pay the bills
- ☐ empty the wastebaskets
- ☐ take out the trash
- ☐ wash the car
- ☐ mow the lawn
- ☐ vacuum the carpets
- ☐ polish the furniture

| Word Work | Partners |

Ask a partner about his/her activities last weekend. What chores did he/she do? Circle your partner's answer.

A: **Did you do the laundry?** B: **Yes, I did. I went to the laundromat.**

1. do the laundry	Yes	No	6. change the sheets	Yes	No
2. cook	Yes	No	7. take out the trash	Yes	No
3. pay the bills	Yes	No	8. wash the car	Yes	No
4. dust	Yes	No	9. weed the garden	Yes	No
5. vacuum the carpets	Yes	No	10. mow the lawn	Yes	No

Cleaning Supplies

A Write the name of the cleaning item and one cleaning supply you associate with it.

1. _____*sponge*_____   2. _____   3. _____

_____*dishwashing soap*_____   _____   _____

4. _____   5. _____   6. _____

_____   _____   _____

B Write the word for each cleaning supply.

1. rubber _____*gloves*_____   5. paper _____

2. scrub _____   6. recycling _____

3. glass _____   7. trash _____

4. bug _____   8. scouring _____

C Complete the sentences.

1. You sweep the floor with a _____*broom*_____.

2. You kill flies with a _____.

3. You catch mice with a _____.

4. You wear _____ when you wash the dishes in hot water.

5. You put a _____ in a trash can.

6. You stand on a _____ to reach a high shelf.

7. You put empty cans and bottles in a _____.

D Complete the questions with the name of a cleaning supply.

1. ___Do we have any dishwasher detergent___ for the dishwasher?

2. _____ for the vacuum cleaner?

3. _____ to wash the windows?

4. _____ to catch those mice?

5. _____ to polish the furniture?

6. _____ to clean the sink?

7. _____ to wash the dishes?

8. _____ to kill those ants?

CD 1
Track 41

E Listen to each request. Circle the correct response.

1. **(a.)** Where's the vacuum cleaner?   **b.** Where's the mop?

2. **a.** Where's the dish soap?   **b.** Where's the furniture polish?

3. **a.** Where's the bug spray?   **b.** Where's the dish soap?

4. **a.** Where's the dust mop?   **b.** Where's the flyswatter?

5. **a.** Where's the squeegee?   **b.** Where's the scouring pad?

6. **a.** Where's the cleanser?   **b.** Where's the dustpan?

7. **a.** Where's the bucket?   **b.** Where's the broom?

Word Study

Put sticky notes on some of the items in your home. Look at the items several times a day and say the words out loud.

Fruits and Nuts

A Complete the sentences with the name of a fruit or nut. Some statements have many possible answers.

1. A _____ peach _____ has a large pit.

2. A _____ is the largest fruit.

3. _____ grow under the ground.

4. _____ and _____ are two kinds of berries.

5. You peel a _____.

6. An _____ and a _____ are two citrus fruits.

7. Two tropical fruits are a _____ and a _____.

8. _____ and _____ grow in my country.

9. My favorite fruit is _____.

B Write two kinds of fruit for each category.

1. These fruits grow on trees: _____ avocado _____   _____ lemon _____

2. These fruits are ice cream flavors: _____   _____

3. You can eat the skin of these fruits: _____   _____

4. You can't eat the skin of these fruits: _____   _____

5. These fruits are good in pies: _____   _____

6. These fruits make delicious juices: _____   _____

C Circle the two words that can follow each word or expression.

1. Canned: lemons   (peaches)   (pears)

2. Dried: apples   cantaloupe   bananas

3. Juicy: avocados   oranges   plums

4. Peel a: mango   strawberry   banana

5. Crack open a: pistachio   walnut   cherry

D **Write the names of the fruit in the produce section of the farmers' market.**

Lemons 50¢

CD 1
Track 42

E **Listen as the two workers put today's prices on the fruit at the farmers' market in Exercise D. Write the price of each fruit.**

Word Work **Partners**

You are making a fruit salad for your family. Write the recipe.

_____

_____

_____

_____

_____

_____

Vegetables

A Write the name of each vegetable.

1. _____ 2. _____ 3. _____ 4. _____

5. _____ 6. _____ 7. _____ 8. _____

B Read the description. Write the name of the correct vegetable from Exercise A.

1. These small, red vegetables are good in salads and soups. In many countries, people cook them with onions and other seasonings. ___*kidney beans*___

2. This round vegetable is dark red. You cannot eat it raw. You must cook it first.

   _____

3. People make pasta sauce with this red vegetable. _____

4. This small vegetable is flavorful and gives a strong taste to sauces, soups, and other foods. _____

5. This vegetable can be red, green, or yellow. The inside is hollow (empty). People use this vegetable in salads and stir-fries, or they stuff it with rice, meat, or other vegetables. _____

6. This green vegetable is the main ingredient in many salads. _____

7. This popular vegetable can be baked, boiled, mashed, or french fried.

   _____

8. This long, orange vegetable grows under the ground. _____

C Circle the vegetables that you can peel.

(carrots)   asparagus   lettuce   squash

spinach   beets   eggplant   green beans

mushrooms   broccoli   sweet potatoes   peas

CD 1
Track 43

D Listen to two friends plan a salad for dinner. Circle the items they will include in the salad.

Word Work **Partners**

Start with lettuce. What other vegetables do you like in a salad? Write a salad recipe with vegetables you both like.

_____

_____

_____

_____

_____

Meat, Poultry, and Seafood

A Write three cuts of meat that come from each animal.

drumsticks _____   _____   _____

_____   _____   _____

_____   _____   _____

B Unscramble each word. Write the kind or cut of meat.

1. laasmi   _____salami_____   6. ahm   _____

2. segl   _____   7. gsinw   _____

3. brsi   _____   8. sssgaaeu _____

4. teaks   _____   9. keyrut   _____

5. cudk   _____   10. cckenih   _____

C Complete the crossword puzzle.

Across

3

6

7

8

Down

1   2    4    5

D Complete the sentences with a kind of meat, poultry, or seafood.

1. I have never tried _____.

2. How do you like your steak? I like it _____.

3. At times, it's difficult to find _____ in the supermarket.

4. Lean meat is healthier for you than _____ meat.

5. Seafood is healthier than _____ because it contains very little fat.

6. _____ is my favorite meat.

7. _____ is my favorite seafood.

CD 1
Track 44

E Complete the sentences with the meat, poultry, or seafood you hear.

1. We're having _____ francése tonight.

2. The special tonight is _____.

3. I'd like a _____ sandwich.

4. A _____ sandwich, please.

5. We're having _____ for dinner tonight.

6. I'll cook some _____ on the grill.

7. I'm going to make meatballs with this _____.

8. The _____ in that restaurant are delicious.

9. My brother is a fisherman. He often brings home fresh _____.

Word Work **Partners**

Which kind of meat, poultry, or seafood do you like best? Compare your answers with your partner.

1. I like _____ salad.

2. I like _____ sandwiches.

3. I like _____ soup.

4. I like _____ on the grill.

Inside the Refrigerator

A Write the names of eight dairy products in the refrigerator in the dictionary.

_____milk_____   _____

_____   _____

_____   _____

_____   _____

> Dairy products are
> made from milk.

B Match the question and answer.

_c_   **1.** What kind of soda do you drink?

____   **2.** What kind of ice cream do you like?

____   **3.** What kind of cold cuts do you like?

____   **4.** What kind of cheese do you buy?

____   **5.** What kind of juice do you drink?

____   **6.** What kind of salad dressing do you buy?

____   **7.** What kind of jam do you buy?

____   **8.** What kind of frozen vegetables do you buy?

____   **9.** What kind of milk do you drink?

____ **10.** What kind of salad do you like?

a. ham and roast beef

b. cheddar

c. cola

d. grape and strawberry

e. vanilla

f. skim

g. potato

h. peas and green beans

i. orange

j. Italian

C Draw a line from each item to the correct label of ingredients.

mayonnaise

ketchup

dressing

yogurt

soda

Carbonated water, corn syrup, sugar, caramel color, caffeine

Oil, eggs, vinegar, salt, sugar, lemon juice

Milk, sugar, strawberries

Tomatoes, vinegar, corn syrup, salt, spices

Water, vinegar, oil, sugar, seasonings

D **Complete the sentences.**

1. I sometimes eat _____ for breakfast.

2. When I'm thirsty, I like to drink _____ .

3. _____ is good for dessert.

4. I put _____ on my salad.

5. I put _____ on waffles.

6. I like _____ eggs.

7. I like _____ cheese.

8. I sometimes have _____ salad for dinner.

9. I have never eaten _____ .

E **Listen to this couple write a list of items they need to buy at the supermarket. Check *Buy* or *Don't buy*.**

CD 1
Track 45

	Buy	Don't buy
1. mayonnaise	✓	
2. yogurt		✓
3. eggs		
4. syrup		
5. cheese		
6. salad dressing		
7. milk		
8. jam		
9. ice cream		

Word Work **Partners**

Circle the items you have in your refrigerator. Write the names of three more items in your refrigerator.

milk	cheese	tofu	_____
eggs	mayonnaise	cold cuts	_____
yogurt	soda	butter	_____

Food to Go

A **Circle the correct word.**

1. I'd like a (straw (slice)) of pizza.

2. I'd like two (tacos   beans).

3. An order of refried (beans   donuts), please.

4. I need (a straw   ketchup) for my soda.

5. I'd like some (ketchup   tea) for my hamburger.

6. A small order of (mustard   french fries) with my hamburger, please.

7. I'd like (tea   salsa) to drink.

8. What kind of (rice   muffin) would you like, corn or blueberry?

9. I'd like milk and sugar in my (spaghetti   coffee).

B **Complete the sentences about the calories and fat in these foods.**

(one cup)   (per roll)   (per slice)

Calories:	140	440	300	290	310
Fat (mg):	5	21	11	10	18

1. A hamburger has _____ calories.

2. Two slices of pizza have _____ calories.

3. Two egg rolls have _____ calories.

4. A hamburger has _____ mg of fat.

5. Two cups of spaghetti have _____ mg of fat.

6. A slice of pizza has more calories than _____.

7. A hot dog has less fat than _____.

8. The healthiest choice for lunch is _____.

C Look at the menu. Figure out the cost of each order below.

Debbie's Diner			
Hamburger	$5.00	Muffin	$2.00
Hot Dog	$3.00	Donut	$1.25
Fish and Chips	$8.00	Bagel	$1.50
Chicken Sandwich	$6.00	Coffee	$1.00
Ham Sandwich	$6.50	Tea	$1.00
French Fries	$2.00	Soda	$1.25

1. _____ 2. _____ 3. _____

CD 1
Track 46

D Listen to each question. Circle the letter of the correct response.

1. **a.** black   **b.** a tortilla

2. **a.** ketchup   **b.** a straw

3. **a.** medium   **b.** salsa

4. **a.** fried   **b.** large

5. **a.** soy sauce   **b.** tea

6. **a.** chopsticks   **b.** french fries

7. **a.** salsa   **b.** a burrito

8. **a.** large   **b.** baked

Word Work **Small Group**

Discuss or write the answers.
1. What fast food restaurants are in this area?
2. How often do you eat at a fast food restaurant?
3. What is your favorite fast food restaurant?
4. What do you usually order there?

Cooking

A **Complete the sentences.**

| Grate | Grease | Puree | Simmer |
| Roast | ~~Season~~ | Sauté | Slice |

1. _____Season_____ the chicken with salt and pepper.

2. _____ the onions with a sharp knife.

3. _____ the turkey for three hours at 350°.

4. _____ the soup for two hours.

5. _____ the onions and peppers in oil in a frying pan.

6. _____ the strawberries, milk, and yogurt in a blender.

7. _____ 1/2 cup of cheddar cheese.

8. _____ two cake pans.

B **Read the directions. Check *Possible* or *Not possible*.**

	Possible	Not possible
1. Peel the lettuce.	____	✓
2. Bake the cake.	____	____
3. Boil the cookies.	____	____
4. Slice the tomato.	____	____
5. Sift the strawberries.	____	____
6. Scramble the eggs.	____	____
7. Measure the flour.	____	____

C **Write a food that you prepare each way.**

1. I grill _____. 3. I microwave _____.

2. I roast _____. 4. I marinate _____.

5. I bake _____.

7. I simmer _____.

6. I steam _____.

8. I broil _____.

D **Circle the correct directions in the recipe.**

Blueberry Banana Pancakes

2 cups pancake mix   2 eggs

1 large banana   3 tablespoons oil

1 3/4 cups milk   1 cup blueberries

((Grease)   Season) a large frying pan. (Marinate   Puree) the banana in a blender for 30 seconds. (Cook   Add) the eggs, milk, and oil and puree for 30 more seconds. Put the pancake mix into a large bowl. (Whisk   Peel) the wet and dry ingredients together. Gently (sift   stir) in the blueberries. (Cook   Roast) the pancakes for one to two minutes on each side. Top the pancakes with more blueberries.

CD 1
Track 47

E **Listen and complete the recipe.**

Chili

1 onion   2 teaspoons cumin

1 tablespoon olive oil   1 1/2 cups of crushed tomatoes

1 pound ground beef   1 15-ounce can kidney beans

2 tablespoons chili powder

1. _____Chop_____ the onion. _____ in olive oil for five minutes.

2. _____ the ground beef and _____ for five more minutes.

3. _____ the chili powder and cumin.

4. _____ in the tomatoes and beans. _____ for twenty minutes.

Word Work **Small Group**

People prepare rice many different ways. Write or explain one of your family's favorite recipes with rice.

Cooking Equipment

A Look in your dictionary. Check the location of each item.

	on the wall	on a shelf	on the island	on the stove
hand mixer	___	___	✓	___
mixing bowl	___	___	___	___
wok	___	___	___	___
grill	___	___	___	___
cake pan	___	___	___	___
frying pan	___	___	___	___
casserole	___	___	___	___

B Look in your dictionary. Complete the names of the cooking equipment.

1. a cutting _____

2. a vegetable _____

3. _____ cups

4. a can _____

5. a cookie _____

6. a cake _____

7. a set of _____

8. a mixing _____

C Ask about the location of the item you need for each job.

1. Please open this can.   _Where is the can opener?_____

2. Please peel the carrots.   _____

3. Please grate the cheese.   _____

4. I need one teaspoon of salt.   _____

5. This needs to cook for one hour. _____

6. Please turn the hamburgers.   _____

7. I need a half cup of flour.   _____

8. Please cut the potatoes.   _____

9. Please open this bottle.   _____

D Write five items from your dictionary in each group.

I use this item every day.	I use this item once a week.	I seldom use this item.
_____	_____	_____
_____	_____	_____
_____	_____	_____
_____	_____	_____
_____	_____	_____

CD 1
Track 48

E Listen to each statement. Write the number of the correct item under each picture.

a. _____

b. _____

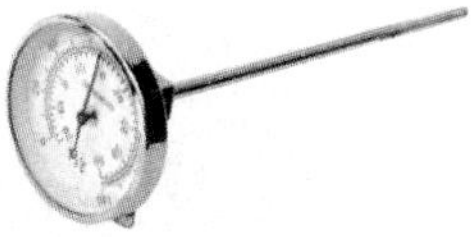

c. _____

d. _____

e. _____

f.  1

g. _____

h. _____

Word Work Small Group

You are making the following items. List the cooking equipment you will need.

A cake: _____

_____

Scrambled eggs: _____

_____

Measurements and Containers

A Write the word for each item. Use a measure or container.

1. _a bunch of bananas_   2. _____   3. _____

4. _____   5. _____   6. _____

7. _____   8. _____   9. _____

B Cross out the measurement or container that cannot hold each item.

1. flowers: ~~bar~~   bouquet   bunch   basket

2. soda: can   six-pack   tray   bottle

3. potatoes: bag   tube   basket   crate

4. cookies: box   tray   quart   bag

5. tea: basket   cup   pot   container

6. oranges: pile   basket   jar   crate

7. water: gallon   bag   quart   cup

8. flour: bag   gallon   cup   teaspoon

C Complete the sentences with a container. There are several correct answers.

1. We don't have any milk. <u>I'll buy a quart.</u>

2. We don't have any soup. _____

3. We don't have any blueberries. _____

4. We don't have any bread. _____

5. We don't have any rice. _____

6. We don't have any apple juice. _____

7. We don't have any mayonnaise. _____

D Circle the amount that is larger.

1. **a.** one teaspoon (**b.**) one tablespoon

2. **a.** one cup **b.** one tablespoon

3. **a.** one pint **b.** one cup

4. **a.** one cup **b.** one quart

5. **a.** one quart **b.** one ounce

6. **a.** one gallon **b.** one quart

7. **a.** one cup **b.** one liter

CD 1
Track 49

E Listen to each question. Circle the amount each person should buy.

1. (**a.**) one quart **b.** one basket   5. **a.** one loaf **b.** one jar

2. **a.** two bunches **b.** two bars   6. **a.** one six-pack **b.** one tray

3. **a.** one bag **b.** one bottle   7. **a.** one piece **b.** one carton

4. **a.** two pots **b.** two pounds   8. **a.** four crates **b.** four containers

Word Work | **Partners**

How much of each item do you usually buy each week?

Who buys more of each item?

1. milk   3. bread   5. eggs

2. soda   4. juice   6. rice

Supermarket

A Look at the picture of the supermarket in the dictionary.
Circle *T* if the statement is true. Circle *F* if the statement is false.

1. There are six aisles in the supermarket.   T   (F)

2. The deli counter is on the right.   T   F

3. There is a scale on the deli counter.   T   F

4. The produce department is in the back.   T   F

5. Six customers are using shopping carts.   T   F

6. The three cashiers are busy.   T   F

7. The bagger is putting the groceries in a plastic bag. T   F

B Add one more item to each section of a supermarket.

1. canned goods: soup   _____

2. dairy products: yogurt   _____

3. frozen foods: ice cream   _____

4. bakery: cake   _____

5. deli counter: potato salad   _____

6. paper products: toilet paper   _____

7. household cleaners: dish soap   _____

C Complete the story.

Sylvia stopped at the supermarket yesterday to shop for groceries for dinner. In the ___*produce*___ section, she chose some tomatoes and lettuce. In the _____ section, she bought some chicken. She stopped in the _____ aisle for soda. In the _____ section, she picked up milk and cheese. She also stopped in the _____ aisle to buy toilet paper and napkins. The supermarket wasn't busy, so she didn't have to wait in line. She put her groceries on the _____. The cashier used the _____ to scan her items. The _____ put her groceries in two _____ bags.

D **Put the steps in order.**

_____ The customer pays the cashier.

_1_ The customer takes a shopping cart.

_____ The bagger puts the groceries in plastic or paper bags.

_____ The customer walks up and down the aisles and shops for groceries.

_____ The customer goes to the checkout counter.

_____ The cashier uses a barcode scanner to total the groceries.

CD 1
Track 50

E **Listen to a customer ask about the location of each item. Circle the letter of the correct section.**

1. (**a.**) pet food   **b.** beverages   **c.** bakery

2. **a.** canned goods   **b.** paper products   **c.** deli counter

3. **a.** dairy products   **b.** frozen foods   **c.** household cleaners

4. **a.** paper products   **b.** canned goods   **c.** deli counter

5. **a.** produce   **b.** dairy products   **c.** meats and poultry

6. **a.** pet food   **b.** beverages   **c.** meats and poultry

7. **a.** produce   **b.** canned goods   **c.** paper products

8. **a.** deli counter   **b.** bakery   **c.** frozen foods

Word Work **Small Group**

Discuss or write the answers.
1. How often do you go to the supermarket?
2. Which supermarket do you usually shop at?
3. Does it have a good produce section?
4. Does it have a bakery?
5. What kind of snacks do you sometimes buy?
6. Does the supermarket have barcode scanners at the checkout counters?

Restaurant

A Look in your dictionary. Write each word in the correct group.

bowl	~~appetizer~~	dessert	waiter
waitress	glass	main course	cup
plate	busser	chef	salad

The Meal	People	Dishes
appetizer		

B Read the instructions for setting a dinner table. Did the person who set the table follow the instructions? Circle *Yes* or *No*.

1. Put the dinner plate in the center of the setting.	(Yes)	No
2. Put the soup bowl on the dinner plate.	Yes	No
3. Put the knife next to the plate, on the right.	Yes	No
4. Put the soup spoon to the right of the knife.	Yes	No
5. Put the dinner fork next to the plate, on the left.	Yes	No
6. Put the salad fork to the left of the dinner fork.	Yes	No
7. Put the napkin to the left of the fork.	Yes	No
8. Put the water glass above the knife.	Yes	No
9. Put a saltshaker and a pepper shaker on every table.	Yes	No

c **Listen and write the name of the item that each customer is requesting.**

CD 1
Track 51

1. _____ high chair _____   6. _____

2. _____   7. _____

3. _____   8. _____

4. _____   9. _____

5. _____   10. _____

Word Work **Partners**

Put the restaurant items in pairs. Explain why the items belong together.

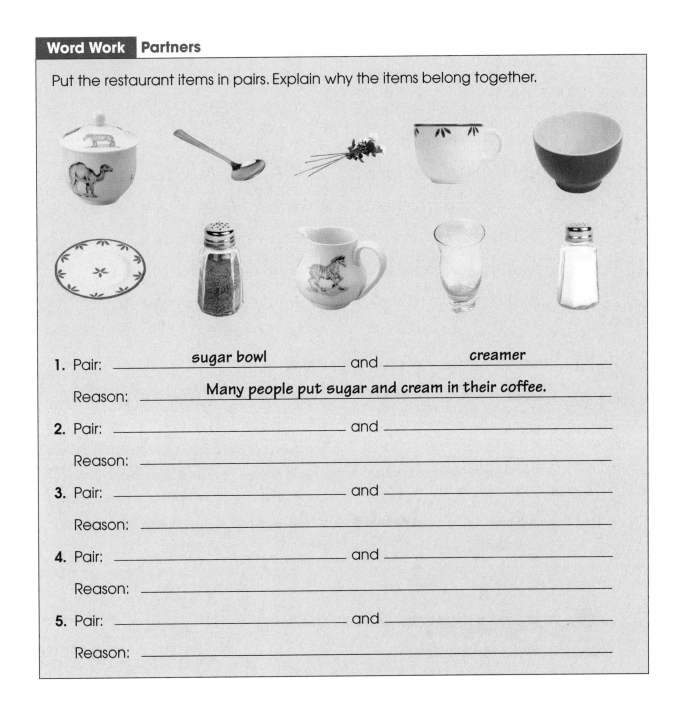

1. Pair: _____ sugar bowl _____ and _____ creamer _____

   Reason: _____ Many people put sugar and cream in their coffee. _____

2. Pair: _____ and _____

   Reason: _____

3. Pair: _____ and _____

   Reason: _____

4. Pair: _____ and _____

   Reason: _____

5. Pair: _____ and _____

   Reason: _____

Order, Eat, Pay

A **Circle the letter of the sentence with the same meaning.**

1. A waitress is putting dishes and glasses on a table.

   (a.) She's setting the table.   **b.** She's clearing the table.

2. A customer is deciding what to order for dinner.

   a. He's taking an order.   **b.** He's looking at the menu.

3. A waiter is giving each person his or her order.

   a. He's setting the table.   **b.** He's serving the meal.

4. A waiter is pouring more water in the glasses on the table.

   a. He's refilling the glasses.   **b.** He's spilling the water.

5. A waiter is cleaning the table with a cloth.

   a. He's spilling a drink.   **b.** He's wiping the table.

6. Two customers are eating a piece of cake.

   a. They're ordering dessert.   **b.** They're sharing dessert.

B **Circle two words that can follow each verb.**

1. pour: (water)   a meal   (coffee)

2. serve: a meal   a dessert   a tip

3. compliment: the waiter   the cook   the check

4. spill: a reservation   a drink   coffee

5. ask for: the check   a menu   a customer

6. refill: the water   the coffee   the table

C **Amy is at a restaurant. What is she doing?**

1. "The food is delicious."   _She's complimenting the chef._

2. "I'm leaving the waiter $10."   _____

3. "I'd like a table for two people for 7:00."   _____

4. "I'd like the check, please." _____

5. "Here's my credit card." _____

6. "I'd like a salad and steak." _____

7. "A piece of cake and two forks, please." _____

CD 1
Track 52

D **Listen to the story of Luis's first night as a waiter. Then, read each statement and circle *True* or *False*.**

1. Mr. and Mrs. Park made a reservation at the restaurant. (True) False

2. Luis waited on Mr. and Mrs. Park. True False

3. Mr. Park ordered a large pizza with sausage. True False

4. Luis spilled water on the table. True False

5. Mr. Park complimented the waiter. True False

6. The manager thanked the server. True False

7. Mr. Park paid the check. True False

8. Mr. Park left a big tip for Luis. True False

Word Work **Small Group**

Discuss or write the answers.

1. How often do you eat out?
2. What kind of food do you like?
3. What is your favorite restaurant in this area?
4. How is the service?
5. Do you sometimes share a salad or dessert?
6. Did you ever take home a doggie bag?
7. How much tip do you leave for the server?

Word Study

It is normal to try to translate new words into your first language. After you hear a word a few times, form a relationship between the word and the picture in your mind. For example, after you learn the word "vase," don't continue to translate the word. Try to see a picture of a vase with flowers in it.

Clothes

A Circle the clothes people wear when it's cold outside.

(a sweater)   a jacket   a T-shirt   a hat

a coat   shorts   a gown   a scarf

a trench coat   a sweatshirt   a shawl   a poncho

B Circle the correct word.

1. When it's raining, I wear a ((raincoat)   tie).

2. When I exercise, I wear a sweatshirt and (a skirt   sweatpants).

3. A police officer wears a (blouse   uniform) to work.

4. Wear a blue (sari   tie) with that shirt.

5. When it is windy, I wear a (vest   windbreaker).

6. When it's cool outside, I put on a light (jacket   tuxedo).

7. Many people wear (hats   ponchos) to protect their skin from the hot sun.

8. It's going to be a formal party. You should wear (a dress   jeans).

C In your notebook, write a description of the clothes that each person is wearing.

1.

2.

3.

4.

5.

6.

D Read each statement. Check *Good idea* or *Bad idea*.

	Good idea	Bad idea
1. It's raining, so I'm wearing a raincoat.	✓	___
2. It's cold, so I'm wearing shorts.	___	___
3. It's hot, so I'm wearing a T-shirt.	___	___
4. My brother is getting married, so he's wearing blue jeans.	___	___
5. I'm exercising, so I'm wearing a suit.	___	___
6. My aunt is pregnant, so she's wearing a maternity dress.	___	___
7. I'm going to work, so I'm wearing my uniform.	___	___
8. I have a job interview, so I'm wearing sweatpants.	___	___
9. I'm riding a bike, so I'm wearing a skirt.	___	___
10. My sister is getting married, so she's wearing a gown.	___	___

 CD 2 Track 1

E Listen to each speaker. Number the two items each person bought.

a. _____   b. _____   c. _____   d. _____   e. _____1

f. _____   g. _____   h. _____   i. _____1   j. _____

Word Work | **Small Group**

Discuss or write the answers.
1. What clothing stores do you shop at?
2. When is the last time you went to a clothing store?
3. What did you buy?
4. How much money did you spend?

Sleepwear, Underwear, and Swimwear

A **Circle the items that come in pairs.**

(socks)   slip   camisole   boxer shorts

nylons   swimsuit   panties   stockings

tank top   tights   bikini   pajamas

B **Look at the clothesline in the dictionary. Answer the questions.**

1. What color is the T-shirt?   It's white.

2. What color are the flip flops?   _____

3. What color is the leotard?   _____

4. What color are the briefs?   _____

5. What color are the slippers?   _____

6. What color is the bathrobe?   _____

7. What color is the slip?   _____

8. What color are the pajamas?   _____

C **Add three items to each group.**

Men's Underwear	Women's Underwear
tank top	girdle
_____	_____
_____	_____
_____	_____

D **Complete the sentences.**

1. Women wear a _____ slip _____ under a dress.

2. Men usually wear a _____ under a dress shirt.

3. When it is cold, little children often wear a _____ to bed.

4. Dancers usually wear a _____ and _____.

5. Men usually sleep in _____.

6. Women usually sleep in a _____ or _____.

7. People wear _____ with their sneakers.

8. A man wears _____ when he swims.

9. A woman wears a _____ or a _____ when she swims.

10. When it's very cold, people who work outside often wear _____ under their clothes.

E **Match the questions and answers.**

_c_ 1. Do you wear tights?

_____ 2. Do you wear a bikini?

_____ 3. Do you wear slippers at the beach?

_____ 4. Do you wear briefs?

_____ 5. Do you wear pajamas?

_____ 6. Do you wear a tank top under a dress shirt?

a. No, I wear a nightshirt.

b. No, I wear boxers.

c. No, I wear pantyhose.

d. No, I wear an undershirt.

e. No, I wear flip flops.

f. No, I wear a bathing suit.

CD 2
Track 2

F **Listen and write the correct price under each item.**

a. $ _____

b. $23 _____

c. $ _____

d. $ _____

e. $ _____

f. $ _____

g. $ _____

h. $ _____

Word Work **Partners**

Look in your dictionary. Make a list of five items that you can put in the dryer.
Make a list of five items that you should hang on a clothesline.

Shoes and Accessories

A Write the names of eight accessories that this woman is wearing or carrying.

1. _____ ring _____
2. _____
3. _____
4. _____
5. _____
6. _____
7. _____
8. _____

B Write the names of eight items that come in pairs.

1. a pair of ___ sandals ___
2. a pair of _____
3. a pair of _____
4. a pair of _____
5. a pair of _____
6. a pair of _____
7. a pair of _____
8. a pair of _____

C Tell each person what kind of shoes to wear.

1. For a hike in the mountains, wear ___ hiking boots ___.
2. For a day at the beach, wear _____.
3. For a run in the park, wear _____.
4. With a business suit, a man should wear _____.
5. For a formal party, a woman should wear _____.
6. When it's snowing hard, you should wear _____.
7. With a business suit, a woman should wear _____.

D Complete the sentences.

1. I stand all day at work, so I wear ___comfortable___ shoes.

2. When James asked Kathy to marry him, he gave her an _____.

3. What time is it? I can't find my _____.

4. It's cold outside. Wear your _____ and your _____.

5. I don't have pierced ears, so I have to wear _____.

6. My dad doesn't like belts, so he wears _____.

7. It's going to be sunny at the beach today. Wear your _____.

8. A businessman or businesswoman carries papers in a _____.

E Listen to the conversation between a mother and her daughter. Match the item and the location.

CD 2
Track 3

___b___ 1. pumps   **a.** in her purse

_____ 2. hat and gloves   **b.** in a bag in the car

_____ 3. purse   **c.** next to the TV

_____ 4. wallet   **d.** in the car

_____ 5. briefcase   **e.** on the table

_____ 6. sunglasses   **f.** in her coat pocket

_____ 7. key chain   **g.** on the desk

Word Work **Partners**

Dress up this young man. Draw and label the shoes and accessories he is wearing.

Describing Clothes

A | **Match the clothes and the statement.**

　　a.　　　　　　　b.　　　　　　　c.　　　　　　　d.　　　　　　　e.

1. She's wearing a straight skirt. _b_

2. She's wearing a pleated skirt. ____

3. She's wearing a long skirt. ____

4. She's wearing a tight skirt. ____

5. She's wearing a short skirt. ____

6. She's wearing a cardigan sweater. ____

7. She's wearing a polo shirt. ____

8. She's wearing a turtleneck sweater. ____

9. She's wearing a crew neck sweater. ____

10. She's wearing a V-neck sweater. ____

B | **Write a response for each question, beginning with _No_.**

1. Should I wear a pleated skirt? _____ No, wear a straight skirt. _____

2. Should I wear a long-sleeved shirt? _____

3. Should I wear casual clothes? _____

4. Should I wear a narrow tie? _____

5. Should I wear a heavy jacket? _____

6. Should I wear a short skirt? _____

7. Should I wear high heels? _____

8. Should I wear flared jeans? _____

C Describe the clothes each person is wearing.

1   2   3   4

1. ___She's wearing a white V-neck blouse and a straight black skirt.___

2. _____

_____

3. _____

_____

4. _____

_____

CD 2
Track 4

D Listen to this young woman decide which clothes to wear. Match the clothes that she is going to wear.

Word Work Partners

Choose three pictures from a magazine. Describe the clothes that the people are wearing.

Fabrics and Patterns

A Unscramble each word. What is the fabric?

1. ertheal _____leather_____
2. loow _____
3. imden _____
4. oottcn _____
5. nonly _____

6. sherecam _____
7. nilne _____
8. ceal _____
9. tevlev _____
10. deeus _____

B Circle the letter of the item that you can buy in a clothing store.

1. **a.** corduroy pajamas   **(b.)** silk pajamas

2. **a.** a wool sweater   **b.** a denim sweater

3. **a.** leather shoes   **b.** cashmere shoes

4. **a.** lace tie   **b.** silk tie

5. **a.** a wool hat   **b.** a lace hat

6. **a.** a cotton T-shirt   **b.** a leather T-shirt

7. **a.** a velvet robe   **b.** a nylon robe

8. **a.** linen jeans   **b.** denim jeans

C Complete the sentences. There are many possible answers.

1. A cashmere sweater is more expensive than ____a wool sweater____.

2. A wool jacket is less expensive than _____.

3. A velvet robe is softer than _____.

4. A silk tie is more fashionable than _____.

5. A wool sweater is warmer than _____.

6. Corduroy pants are heavier than _____.

7. A lace dress is more formal than _____.

8. A wool scarf is warmer than _____.

D Write the pattern under each scarf.

1. ___solid___

2. _____

3. _____

4. _____

5. _____

6. _____

7. _____

8. _____

CD 2
Track 5

E Listen to each conversation. Write the name of the pattern that the woman chooses under each picture.

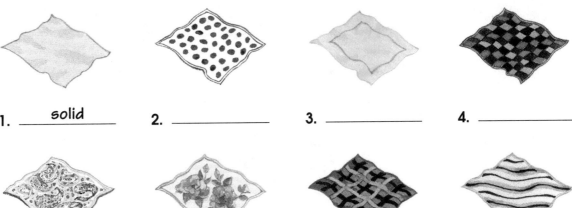

Conversation 1:   Conversation 2:   Conversation 3:

_____   _____   _____

Word Work	**Partners**

Plan an outfit for each of these situations. Describe the clothing, the fabric, and the pattern.

1. Business meeting (man): ___a navy wool suit with a polka dot silk tie___

2. Guest at a wedding (woman): _____

3. Teenage boy going to the movies on a cold day: _____

_____

4. Woman on a job interview: _____

113

Buying, Wearing, and Caring for Clothes

A Write two verbs you can associate with each picture.

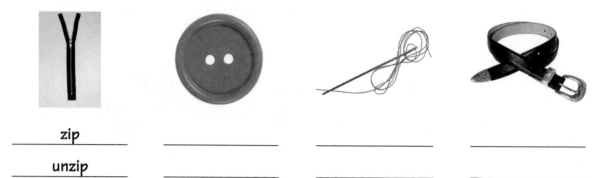

_____zip_____

_____unzip_____

_____ _____ _____

_____ _____ _____

B Circle the correct word.

1. ((Zip up)   Sew on) your coat.

2. (Buckle   Button) your shirt.

3. (Hang up   Button up) your coat in the closet.

4. (Try on   Iron) the shoes.

5. (Cut off   Roll up) the price tag.

6. (Wash   Dry clean) the shirt in cold water.

7. (Press   Sew on) the button.

C Complete the story using these words.

ironed	~~went shopping~~	hung	unbuttoned	put on
went into	sewed on	bought	tried on	took it home

Peter ____**went shopping**____ for a shirt to wear to a party. He saw three shirts that

he liked. He _____ the dressing room and _____

all three. He _____ the blue one and _____. When

he got home, he _____ the shirt to show his wife. One button was

loose. When he _____ the shirt, the button came off.

His wife _____ the button for him. Peter _____ the

shirt and _____ it in his closet.

D Write the correct response.

Mend it.	Buy it.	Take it off.
Dry clean it.	~~Cut it off.~~	Roll them up.
Sew it on.	Iron it.	Wash it.

1. The price tag is still on my dress. _____Cut it off._____

2. I'm too hot in this sweater. _____

3. I spilled some coffee on my shirt. _____

4. I have a rip in my sleeve. _____

5. My button came off. _____

6. I really like this dress. _____

7. My shirt is wrinkled. _____

8. The sleeves are too long. _____

9. My leather jacket is dirty. _____

CD 2
Track 6

E Listen to each statement. Write the number of the statement under the correct picture.

a. ____   b. ____   c. __1__   d. ____

e. ____   f. ____   g. ____   h. ____

Word Work **Partners**

Write three clothing items that you can wash. Write three clothing items that you have to dry clean.

115

Sewing and Laundry

A Write the word for each part of this dress.

B Read each statement. Check *Possible* or *Not possible*.

	Possible	Not possible
1. Take up a hem.	✓	____
2. Put the pin in the pincushion.	____	____
3. Measure the hem with a thimble.	____	____
4. Put the thread through the needle.	____	____
5. Sew on a sleeve with a safety pin.	____	____
6. Iron the shirt with a hanger.	____	____
7. Cut the thread with scissors.	____	____
8. Sew on a pocket with a sewing machine.	____	____

C Complete the instructions for washing and drying clothes.

1. Turn on the water in the washing machine. Add the ___laundry detergent___ and

   the _____. Put the clothes in the machine.

2. Take the _____ out of the washing machine. Put them in the

   _____.

3. When the clothes are dry, fold them. If some of the clothes are wrinkled, set up

   your _____ and heat up the _____.

D **Read the tags. Check the correct instructions.**

A	B	C	D
Machine wash cold water Tumble dry low Do not iron	Machine wash cold Delicate cycle Line dry only	Machine wash with dark colors warm water Tumble dry low Warm iron if needed	Dry clean only

	A	B	C	D
1. Wash this item in cold water.	✓	✓	___	___
2. Wash this item in warm water.	___	___	___	___
3. Use the delicate cycle.	___	___	___	___
4. You can put this item in the dryer.	___	___	___	___
5. Dry clean this item.	___	___	___	___
6. You can iron this item.	___	___	___	___
7. Don't wash this item with white clothes.	___	___	___	___

CD 2
Track 7

E **Listen and write the number of each statement under the correct shirt.**

a. ___

b. __6__

c. ___

d. ___

e. ___

f. ___

Word Study

It's easy to draw pictures of many items, such as clothing. Choose six words that are difficult for you to remember. Copy the words and draw a picture next to each one to remind you of the word. Repeat the words, trying to remember the picture you drew for each one.

Vehicles and Traffic Signs

A Complete these signs. Write the missing words on the signs.

B Complete the sentences.

1. A bride and groom sometimes rent a _____limousine_____ to take them to their wedding.

2. People in an _____ often stay at a campground.

3. A _____ transports food, appliances, furniture, and other items across the country.

4. A _____ takes children to school.

5. The truck is pulling a _____ with horses in it.

6. You call a _____ if your car breaks down on the highway.

7. Many countries require a _____ rider to wear a helmet.

8. People in a _____ can ride with the top down in good weather.

9. A _____ carries dirt or sand to a construction site.

10. An _____ takes injured people to the hospital.

C When you are driving, you must stop for certain vehicles when their lights are flashing. Write the names of four of these vehicles.

1. _____a police car_____   3. _____

2. _____   4. _____

D Complete the sentences with the names of vehicles. There are many correct answers.

1. ____A limousine____ is more comfortable than ____a pickup truck____.

2. _____ can carry more than _____.

118

3. _____ is faster than _____.

4. _____ gets better gas mileage than _____.

5. _____ is more expensive than _____.

6. _____ is better for a large family than _____.

7. _____ is more useful on a farm than _____.

CD 2
Track 8

E **Listen to each statement. Write the number of the statement under the correct road sign.**

a. _____

b. _____

c. _____

d. _____

e. _1_

f. _____

g. _____

h. _____

i. _____

j. _____

Word Work **Small Group**

Guess the meaning of these road signs.

1.

2.

3.

4.

5.

6.

7.

8.

9.

10.

Parts of a Car

A Write the name of each part of this car.

1. _____
2. _____
3. _____
4. _____
5. _____
6. _____
7. _____
8. _____
9. _____
10. _____

B Complete each sentence with a word from Exercise A.

1. Put the key in the _____ignition_____.

2. Let's listen to some music. Turn on the _____.

3. Honk the _____.

4. Step on the _____. There is a stop sign ahead.

5. You're going too slowly. Step on the _____.

6. When you park on a hill, put on the _____.

7. It's hot in here. Turn on the _____.

8. Use the _____. Put the car in second gear.

9. Look in the _____. See if it's safe to pass.

10. Look at the _____. You're speeding!

C Match to make sentences.

__c__ 1. I don't know how fast I'm going

_____ 2. I can't drive in the rain

_____ 3. I can't listen to music

_____ 4. I don't know if I need gas

_____ 5. I can't see the road behind me

_____ 6. I hope I don't get a flat tire

_____ 7. I don't like to drive when it's hot

a. because the gas gauge doesn't work.

b. because the rearview mirror is missing.

c. because the speedometer is broken.

d. because I don't have a spare tire.

e. because someone stole the radio.

f. because the windshield wipers don't work.

g. because the heater doesn't work.

CD 2
Track 9

D Listen to a father teach his daughter how to drive. Circle the correct statement.

1. **(a.)** Step on the brake.　　　　**b.** Step on the accelerator.

2. **a.** Put on the brake light.　　　**b.** Put on the turn signal.

3. **a.** Take off the gearshift.　　　**b.** Take off the emergency brake.

4. **a.** Honk the horn.　　　　　　**b.** Turn off the ignition.

5. **a.** Check the rearview mirror.　**b.** Check the battery.

6. **a.** Turn on the radiator.　　　　**b.** Turn on the headlights.

7. **a.** Turn on the windshield wipers.　**b.** Turn on the brake light.

Word Work　**Small Group**

Take this driving quiz. Then, discuss your answers with your group.

		True	False
1. You should pass another vehicle on the right.		True	False
2. Driving too slowly can cause an accident.		True	False
3. You can park in front of a fire hydrant.		True	False
4. When you enter a highway, you must yield to traffic.		True	False
5. Cars must stop for a pedestrian in a crosswalk.		True	False
6. You can talk on a hand-held cell phone when driving.		True	False

Road Trip

A **Check the things you should do before you take a road trip.**

_____ **1.** pack

_____ **2.** honk the horn

_____ **3.** get gas

_____ **4.** get a speeding ticket

_____ **5.** check the oil

_____ **6.** put air in the tires

_____ **7.** look at a map and check the directions

_____ **8.** pay a toll

B **Put each group of sentences in order.**

_____ I showed the officer my license and registration.

_____ I got a speeding ticket.

_____ A police officer pulled me over.

__1__ I was speeding.

_____ I got on the highway again.

_____ I was driving on the highway.

_____ I changed the tire.

_____ I pulled over to the side of the road.

_____ I got a flat tire.

C **Complete the story.**

Ben and Joji decided to go to the beach. They _____**packed**_____ their

towels, bathing suits, and a picnic lunch into the car. Before they

_____ the highway, they _____ gas and

_____ the oil. As they were driving, they heard a loud noise. They

_____ a flat tire. Ben _____ to the side of the road.

They _____ the tire and continued along the road. After an hour,

they _____ the toll and _____ the highway. They

_____ at the beach at 11:00. They _____ the car

and carried their things onto the beach.

D **Match. What is this couple going to do?**

_f_ **1.** After they pack the car,

a. they're going to call the police.

_____ **2.** When they get gas,

b. they're going to ask for directions.

_____ **3.** If they get lost,

c. they're going to park the car.

_____ **4.** If they pass a construction area,

d. they're going to check the oil.

_____ **5.** If they have an accident,

e. they're going to get a ticket.

_____ **6.** If they speed,

f. they're going to leave home.

_____ **7.** As they get off the highway,

g. they're going to pay the toll.

_____ **8.** When they arrive at the hotel,

h. they're going to slow down.

CD 2
Track 10

E **Listen to each statement and look at the picture. Circle *True* or *False*.**

Picture 1	**Picture 2**	**Picture 3**
1. (True) False	**1.** True False	**1.** True False
2. True False	**2.** True False	**2.** True False
3. True False	**3.** True False	**3.** True False
4. True False	**4.** True False	**4.** True False

Word Work **Small Group**

Discuss or write the answers. Explain where you were and
what you did in each situation.

1. Did you ever get lost?

2. Did you ever have a flat tire?

3. Did you ever get a ticket?

4. Did you ever have an accident?

5. Did you ever run out of gas?

Airport

A **Complete the sentences.**

1. A plane takes off and lands on a _____runway_____.

2. A _____ flies the plane.

3. Passengers must show a _____ at the ticket counter.

4. Passengers with electronic tickets can use the _____.

5. Passengers pass through a _____ at the security checkpoint.

6. A _____ is a small suitcase that a passenger takes onto the plane.

7. Passengers put their carry-on bags into the _____.

8. A _____ serves drinks and meals.

9. After the flight, passengers pick up their luggage in the _____.

10. Passengers from other countries must pass through _____.

B **Put the sentences in order.**

_____ Stand in line at the security checkpoint.

__1__ Check in and show your photo ID at the ticket counter.

_____ Walk to your gate.

_____ Go through the metal detector.

_____ Get your boarding pass.

_____ Show your boarding pass and photo ID to the security officer.

C **Read each statement. Circle _T_ for True or _F_ for False.**

1. You can buy your ticket at an automated check-in machine.   T   (F)

2. You must show your photo ID when you check in.   T   F

3. First class is more expensive than economy class.   T   F

4. You need to take off a metal belt at the security checkpoint.   T   F

5. You wait for your plane in the baggage claim area.   T   F

6. At customs, the official can check your bags.   T   F

7. All passengers must pass through immigration.   T   F

D In your notebook, write eight sentences about this picture. Use the words below.

1. passengers   **5.** economy class

2. seat   **6.** emergency exit

3. aisle   **7.** carry-on bag

4. seat belt   **8.** overhead compartment

CD 2
Track 11

E Listen to each sentence. Where is each person? Write the number of the statement next to the correct area in the airport.

____ security checkpoint   ____ gate

_1_ customs   ____ baggage claim

____ ticket counter   ____ immigration

| **Word Work** | **Small Group** |

Discuss or write the answers.

1. What is the nearest international airport to your house?

2. What airlines does it serve?

3. How often do you fly?

4. How long are the lines at the security checkpoint?

5. Do you buy airline tickets online or from a travel agent?

Taking a Flight

A In your notebook, write about each picture. What is happening?

1.

2.

3.

4.

5.

6.

B Read the two statements. If the meaning is the same, circle *S.* If the meaning is different, circle *D.*

1. Check in.	Go to the ticket counter.	(S) D
2. Go through security.	Walk through the metal detector.	S D
3. Stow your bag.	Put your bag in the overhead compartment.	S D
4. Board the plane.	Get off the plane.	S D
5. Choose a meal.	Eat your meal.	S D
6. Claim your bag.	Get your bag at the baggage claim area.	S D
7. Fasten your seat belt.	Take off your seat belt.	S D

C Put the sentences in order.

_____ Sit down and fasten your seat belt.

_____ Take off.

__1__ Board the plane.

_____ Stow your carry-on bag.

_____ Find your seat.

D Complete the sentences about an uncomfortable flight.

1. I had to wait one hour to ___go through security___.

2. Our flight was delayed. I _____ for four hours.

3. The plane couldn't _____ because of the bad weather.

4. The overhead compartments were full, so I couldn't _____.

5. I couldn't read my book because I couldn't _____.

6. I decided to sleep. I _____, but there weren't any left.

7. I _____, but they were broken. I couldn't hear any music.

8. After we landed, I tried to _____, but all the luggage went to the wrong airport.

CD 2
Track 12

E Look at the picture and listen to each statement. Write the seat number of the correct passenger.

7A   7B   7C   7D   7E   7F   7G   7H

1. __7B__   3. ____   5. ____   7. ____

2. ____   4. ____   6. ____   8. ____

Word Work Partners

You are on a long international flight. Write three sentences explaining how you will pass the time.

Example: **I will put my seat back, put on my headphones, and listen to music.**

1. _____

2. _____

3. _____

Public Transportation

A **Complete the sentences.**

1. The _____subway_____ runs under the city.

2. If there are no seats, hold onto a pole or a _____.

3. A taxi can only carry three or four _____.

4. Each taxi has a _____ to show the fare.

5. A _____ can carry people and cars across a river.

6. You can buy a train ticket at a _____.

7. Give your ticket to the _____ on the train.

8. A _____ gives information about the train times.

B **Read each statement. Check *Possible* or *Not Possible*.**

	Possible	Not Possible
1. Put a token in the turnstile.	✓	____
2. Wait on the platform for the train.	____	____
3. Give your ticket to the taxi driver.	____	____
4. Look at the meter for your fare.	____	____
5. Wait for the train at the taxi stand.	____	____
6. Get a schedule for the next taxi.	____	____
7. Ride the subway under the city.	____	____

C **Complete the sentences about different kinds of public transportation. There are many correct answers.**

1. A _____train_____ is more comfortable than ____a subway____.

2. A _____ is quieter than _____.

3. A _____ is more expensive than _____.

4. A _____ is faster than _____.

5. A _____ is more crowded than _____.

6. A _____ is more convenient than _____.

D Match the questions and answers.

_d_ 1. Where can I get a taxi?   **a.** I take the bus.

____ 2. What's the fare?   **b.** On the platform.

____ 3. Where do I wait for the train?   **c.** I missed the bus.

____ 4. How do you get to work?   **d.** At the taxi stand.

____ 5. Where's your ticket?   **e.** It's $2.00.

____ 6. Why are you late?   **f.** I catch the 7:25.

____ 7. What train do you take?   **g.** I gave it to the conductor.

CD 2
Track 13

E Listen to each statement. Circle the type of transportation each person is talking about — train, subway, or taxi.

1.   **a.** train   **b.** subway   (**c.**) taxi

2.   **a.** train   **b.** subway   **c.** taxi

3.   **a.** train   **b.** subway   **c.** taxi

4.   **a.** train   **b.** subway   **c.** taxi

5.   **a.** train   **b.** subway   **c.** taxi

6.   **a.** train   **b.** subway   **c.** taxi

7.   **a.** train   **b.** subway   **c.** taxi

Word Work **Small Group**

Discuss or write the answers.
1. When do you take public transportation?
2. Where do you wait?
3. How much is the fare?

Up, Over, Around

A **Circle the correct word.**

1. A bridge goes ((over) under) a river.

2. A subway travels (along under) a city.

3. A plane flies (out of over) an ocean.

4. I rode my bicycle (along between) the river.

5. I swam (behind across) the river.

6. We drove (through between) the city.

7. I walked (over toward) the town.

B **Write the opposite of each sentence.**

1. I drove into the tunnel.   _I drove out of the tunnel._

2. I walked over the bridge.   _____

3. I took a left at the light.   _____

4. We made a right at the sign.   _____

5. They hiked up the mountain.   _____

6. Get onto Route 2 West.   _____

C **Write a direction line for each picture.**

Turn left at the traffic light.

_____

_____

_____

_____

D **Look at the map and complete the directions.**

I am a librarian in the city and I drive to work. My house is on Main Street. I drive

_____*along*_____ Main Street and go _____ the Mill Bridge. After the

bridge, I get on Route 80 South. After I go _____ Blue Lake, I make a

_____ onto Route 10 East. I drive _____ the Midtown Tunnel and

_____ the city. I make a _____ onto 7th Avenue, and then a

_____ into the parking lot. The parking lot is _____ the library.

CD 2
Track 14

E **Listen to the directions to Brook Park. In your notebook, take notes or draw a map. Compare your directions with a friend. Listen again and check the directions.**

Word Work **Partners**

Choose a well-known location in your city, such as the hospital or a museum. Write the directions from your school to that location.

Word Study

Talk to yourself in English. If you are alone, talk out loud. If you are in a store, on a bus, or in another location, "talk" in your head. Use your new vocabulary to describe what you see or what you are doing.

Example: *I'm driving south on Route 21. I'm going over a bridge. I'll get off at Exit 9. I need to stop for gas.*

The Human Body

A **Complete the sentences.**

1. You put a ring on your _____finger_____.

2. You put shoes on your _____.

3. You put a watch on your _____.

4. You put a hat on your _____.

5. You put a belt around your _____.

6. You put gloves on your _____.

7. You put makeup on your _____.

8. You put headphones over your _____.

B **There are five senses. Write the part of the body you use for each one.**

1. hearing: _____ears_____

2. seeing: _____

3. touching: _____

4. tasting: _____

5. smelling: _____

C **Match the organ and its function.**

_g_ 1. liver   **a.** They help us to breathe.

____ 2. lungs   **b.** It helps us to digest food.

____ 3. brain   **c.** It helps us to think and to feel.

____ 4. muscles   **d.** It pumps blood through the body.

____ 5. stomach   **e.** They form the skeleton of the body.

____ 6. bones   **f.** They help to clean the blood.

____ 7. skin   **g.** It processes many substances in the body.

____ 8. heart   **h.** It covers the body.

____ 9. kidneys   **i.** They help us to move the body.

CD 2
Track 15

D **Listen to the directions for each of the three stretches. Complete the directions. Then, write the letter of each exercise under the correct picture.**

A. Lie on your _____back_____ with your _____ bent. Slowly lift your

_____ and then your _____ off the floor. Hold for five seconds.

Slowly lower your _____ to the floor, starting with your _____.

B. Lie on your _____ with your _____ bent. Keep one _____

bent. Raise the other _____ to the ceiling. Hold the _____ with

both _____ and gently pull it toward your _____.

C. Lie on your _____ with your _____ bent. Raise and bend one

_____. Hold the _____ with both _____. With your

_____, make small circles in the air.

1. _____   2. _____   3. _____

Word Work **Partners**

Write four parts of your body you use to perform each action.

_____   _____   _____

_____   _____   _____

_____   _____   _____

_____   _____   _____

Illnesses, Injuries, Symptoms, and Disabilities

A **Look at the picture in your dictionary and complete the sentences.**

1. The woman in the green dress has _____asthma_____.

2. Her little boy has an _____.

3. The girl in the yellow shirt has _____ in her hair.

4. The boy in the orange shirt has _____.

5. The man in the green shirt has a _____ and a _____.

6. The woman in the black sweatshirt and sweatpants has a _____.

7. The man in the yellow shirt has a _____.

8. The man in the blue shirt and dark glasses is _____.

9. The girl in the green shirt is _____ and _____.

10. The delivery person is _____.

B **Match the cause and the illness or injury.**

__c__ 1. I ate too much.

____ 2. I fell asleep on the beach.

____ 3. I touched a hot pot.

____ 4. I slipped on the ice.

____ 5. My new shoes are too tight.

____ 6. I got hit in the face with a ball.

____ 7. I ate strawberries. Now my face and neck are red.

a. I have a burn on my hand.

b. I have a rash.

c. I have a stomachache.

d. I have a bloody nose.

e. I have a bad sunburn.

f. I have a sprained ankle.

g. I have a blister on my foot.

C **Look at the Word Partnerships in your dictionary. Complete with *have* or *feel*.**

1. I ____have____ a sore throat.

2. I _____ dizzy.

3. I _____ a bad cold.

4. I _____ a head cold.

5. I _____ nauseous.

6. I _____ the flu.

D **Circle the correct word.**

1. I caught a ((cold) swollen ankle) from my friend.

2. I fell off my bike and I have a (sunburn   sprained wrist).

3. I got a (bruise   sore throat) when I hit my leg on my desk.

4. First, my daughter had (measles   a blister). Then, my son caught it from her.

5. I drink tea when I have a (swollen ankle   sore throat).

6. Children can easily get (acne   lice) from one another.

7. My son has (mumps   asthma). His face and neck are very swollen.

8. My mother has (measles   arthritis) in her hands and knees.

CD 2
Track 16

E **Listen to six people call in sick to work. Write the number of the conversation you hear next to the correct problem.**

____ **a.** dizzy   ____ **d.** a stomachache

____ **b.** a bad cold   __1__ **e.** the flu

____ **c.** chicken pox   ____ **f.** a sprained wrist

Word Work **Small Group**

Ask each other about the illnesses and injuries in the chart. Talk or write about your experiences.

A: Did you ever have a bloody nose?

B: Yes. I was about nine years old. I had a fight with my brother, and he hit me!

	Name:	Name:	Name:
a bloody nose			
a bee sting			
a sprained wrist			
a rash			
the chicken pox			
the mumps			
the measles			

Hurting and Healing

A Match the picture and the action.

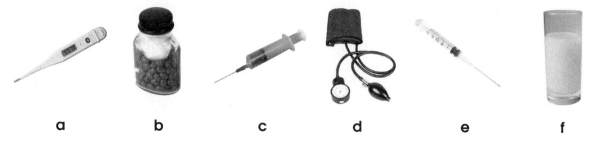

a   b   c   d   e   f

1. The doctor told me to drink a lot of fluids. _____f_____

2. The doctor took my temperature. _____

3. The doctor checked my blood pressure. _____

4. The doctor drew some blood. _____

5. The doctor gave me a shot. _____

6. The doctor told me to take these pills. _____

B Complete the sentences.

had an allergic reaction	drowned	swallowed poison
began to choke	got an electric shock	burned her hand
~~had a heart attack~~	broke my arm	cut my foot

1. He _____**had a heart attack**_____ when he was running a marathon.

2. I _____ when I fell off my bicycle.

3. I _____ when I stepped on a piece of glass.

4. He _____ when he fell out of the boat.

5. He _____ when he was fixing a lamp.

6. She _____ when she was cooking on the grill.

7. He _____ when he was eating a piece of steak.

8. She _____ when she ate some fish.

9. The child _____ when he drank from a bottle of bleach.

C Read the two statements. If the meaning is the same, write *S.* If the meaning is different, write *D.*

1. **a.** He took the pills.   **b.** He took the medication.   _S_

2. **a.** He overdosed on drugs.   **b.** He took too many pills.   ____

3. **a.** She burned her hand.   **b.** She cut her hand.   ____

4. **a.** She had a heart attack.   **b.** She went into shock.   ____

5. **a.** The doctor examined the man.   **b.** The doctor checked the man.   ____

6. **a.** He was in pain.   **b.** He was unconscious.   ____

7. **a.** She drank poison.   **b.** She swallowed poison.   ____

8. **a.** Drink fluids.   **b.** Drink liquids.   ____

CD 2
Track 17

D Listen to the conversation between a doctor and a patient. Read each statement and circle *T* for True or *F* for False.

1. The patient is sneezing and coughing.   (T)   F

2. The patient is vomiting.   T   F

3. The doctor examined the patient.   T   F

4. The doctor took her blood pressure.   T   F

5. The doctor took her temperature.   T   F

6. The doctor gave her a shot.   T   F

7. The patient should return to work tomorrow.   T   F

8. The patient should drink a lot of fluids.   T   F

9. The patient should take four pills a day.   T   F

Word Work Partners

This woman is at the doctor's office. She feels terrible. Write a short conversation between this patient and the doctor.

Hospital

A **Look at the picture of the hospital in your dictionary. Complete the sentences.**

1. The ___emergency room___ of this hospital is busy today.

2. The _____ are bringing a patient into the emergency room. The patient is lying on a _____.

3. One of the patients in the emergency room has a bad cut on his leg. He is getting _____.

4. A _____ brought some flowers to a patient.

5. The lab technician took some _____ from the patient's arm.

6. A patient in the intensive care unit has an _____ in his arm.

7. The surgeon is performing an _____.

8. The patient is lying on the _____ in the operating room.

B **Write one or two items you see in each area of the hospital.**

Operating room: ___latex gloves___ _____

Emergency room: _____ _____

Intensive care unit: _____

Patient's room: _____ _____

C **Match.**

__f__ 1. I need a nurse.

____ 2. Is my arm broken?

____ 3. I can walk.

____ 4. What's your blood type?

____ 5. Do you ever give blood?

____ 6. How bad was the cut?

____ 7. The patient needs more fluids.

a. No, you have to sit in the wheelchair.

b. It's B positive.

c. Start an IV.

d. Yes, I donate blood a few times a year.

e. We need to take an X-ray.

f. Press the call button.

g. I needed ten stitches.

D Write about each picture. What happened to each person? What is happening now? What is going to happen?

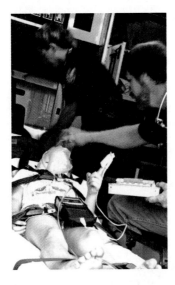
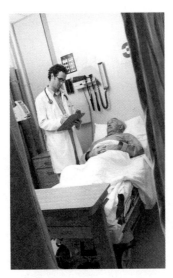
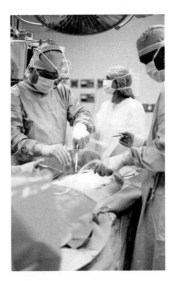

CD 2
Track 18

E Listen to the story about an emergency room patient. Circle *T* if the statement is true. Circle *F* if the statement is false.

1. Henry called for an ambulance.   T   (F)

2. Henry had a bad cut on his leg.   T   F

3. The paramedics started an IV.   T   F

4. The paramedics put Henry in a wheelchair.   T   F

5. Henry went to the intensive care unit.   T   F

6. The doctor ordered an X-ray of Henry's arm.   T   F

7. Henry needed an operation.   T   F

8. Henry needed thirty stitches in his arm.   T   F

Word Work	Small Group

Look at the picture in the dictionary. Use your imagination to discuss or write the answers to these questions.

1. Why is the patient pressing the call button?

2. What happened to the man on the stretcher?

3. What did the lab technician just do?

4. Why does the patient in the emergency room need stitches?

5. What is the relationship between the visitor and the patient?

6. What kind of operation is the surgeon performing?

Medical Center

A Write the name of the specialist that each patient is visiting.

  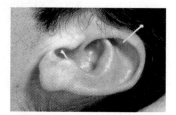

1. _____orthopedist_____   2. _____   3. _____

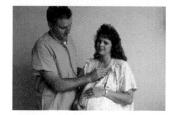  

4. _____   5. _____   6. _____

B Match the specialist and the description.

__g__ 1. psychologist

_____ 2. acupuncturist

_____ 3. pediatrician

_____ 4. cardiologist

_____ 5. obstetrician

_____ 6. orthopedist

_____ 7. general practitioner

_____ 8. optometrist

_____ 9. dental hygienist

_____ 10. dentist

a. a doctor who treats broken bones

b. a doctor who examines eyes

c. a doctor who cares for and treats teeth and gums

d. a doctor who deals with pregnancy and childbirth

e. a doctor who treats diseases and pain with needles

f. a family doctor who practices general medicine

g. a doctor who treats mental and emotional illnesses

h. a person who cleans teeth and assists a dentist

i. a doctor who treats the heart and heart diseases

j. a doctor who treats children

C Complete the sentences with the correct procedure or equipment.

filling	acupuncture	braces	contact lenses
~~EKG~~	crutches	cast	physical

1. You are having some chest pain. You need an _____ EKG _____.

2. Your foot is broken. I need to put it in a _____.

3. You can't walk on that foot for six weeks. You need to use _____.

4. I know you don't like eyeglasses. You could try _____.

5. You have a cavity. You need a _____.

6. Your front teeth are not straight. You need _____.

7. You are a new patient. You will need a complete _____.

8. I always have this pain in my shoulder. I'm going to try _____.

CD 2
Track 19

D Listen to each doctor. Write the number of each statement next to the correct specialist.

_____ **a.** general practitioner

_____ **e.** optometrist

_____ **b.** dentist

_____ **f.** obstetrician

_____ **c.** cardiologist

_____ **g.** orthopedist

_____ **d.** acupuncturist

__1__ **h.** psychologist

Word Work Small Group

These are six other medical specialists. Discuss what they treat or do. Write a definition for each specialist.

podiatrist   dermatologist   plastic surgeon

neurologist   physical therapist   allergist

Example: **A podiatrist is a doctor who treats people's feet.**

Pharmacy

A Write the name of each item.

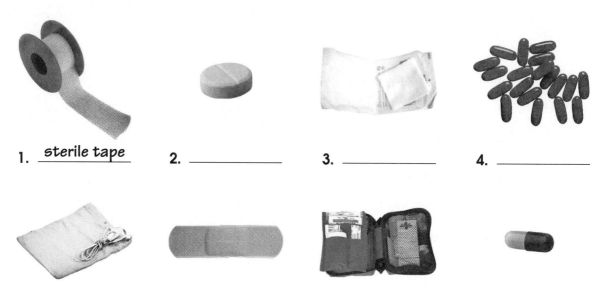

1. _sterile tape_

2. _____

3. _____

4. _____

5. _____

6. _____

7. _____

8. _____

B Read each statement. Check *Good idea* or *Bad idea*.

	Good idea	Bad idea
1. Use an inhaler for allergies.	✓	____
2. Take cough syrup for a toothache.	____	____
3. Take aspirin for a headache.	____	____
4. Use antibacterial ointment for a cut.	____	____
5. Use an ice pack for a sore throat.	____	____
6. Use a humidifier for a cold.	____	____
7. Use a nasal decongestant for a stomachache.	____	____
8. Take vitamins for more energy.	____	____
9. Use a heating pad for a sunburn.	____	____
10. Take lozenges for a backache.	____	____

C Complete the words.

1. nasal _____spray_____

2. hydrogen _____

3. prescription _____

4. warning _____

5. over-the-counter _____

6. knee _____

7. cough _____

8. ice _____

D Give a suggestion for each illness or injury.

1. a cut _____Use antibacterial ointment and an adhesive bandage._____

2. a cold _____

3. a stomachache _____

4. a sore throat _____

5. a fever _____

6. dry eyes _____

7. a cough _____

CD 2
Track 20

E Paul sprained his ankle. Listen to the story. Then, listen to the questions and write the number of each question next to the correct answer.

_____ **a.** He should take aspirin.

_____ **b.** He should use a heating pad.

__1__ **c.** He should use an ice pack.

_____ **d.** He should use a cane.

_____ **e.** He should wear an elastic bandage.

Word Work	Small Group

What do *you* do for each illness or injury?

1. When I have a cold, I _____ .

2. When I have a fever, I _____ .

3. When I have a sore throat, I _____ .

Soap, Comb, and Floss

A Write the names of two products for each part of the body.

1. hair: _____shampoo_____ _____conditioner_____

2. nails: _____ _____

3. teeth: _____ _____

4. skin: _____ _____

5. eyes: _____ _____

B Complete the names of these personal care products.

1. curling ____iron____

2. dental _____

3. face _____

4. eye _____

5. disposable _____

6. shaving _____

7. _____ remover

8. _____ dryer

9. electric _____

10. _____ clipper

C Write a response for each problem or situation.

Use some blush.	Try a curling iron.	Maybe you have a dull razor.
Try this lotion.	~~Use some hairspray.~~	The tissues are on the counter.
Use conditioner.	Put on some sunscreen.	

1. My hair won't stay in place. _____Use some hairspray._____

2. My skin is dry. _____

3. My face is pale. _____

4. The sun is strong today. _____

5. I have a cold. _____

6. My hair is so straight. _____

7. My hair is hard to comb. _____

8. I didn't get a good shave. _____

D Read each sentence. Check *Likely* or *Unlikely.*

	Likely	Unlikely
1. She's washing her hair with sunscreen.	___	✓
2. She's putting blush on her nails.	___	___
3. He's shaving with an electric razor.	___	___
4. She's putting lipstick on her eyelashes.	___	___
5. He's putting deodorant on his hair.	___	___
6. She has a cold. She's using a tissue.	___	___
7. She's brushing her teeth with conditioner.	___	___

CD 2
Track 21

E Listen to Eva's morning routine. Circle the personal care items that she uses.

(toothbrush)	shampoo	curling iron	blush	nail polish
toothpaste	conditioner	lotion	eyeliner	brush
soap	blow dryer	face powder	deodorant	lipstick

Word Study

Use the notecard method.

- Write each word you want to learn on one side of a notecard.
- On the other side, draw a picture of the word or write the word in your language. Also, write a sentence on the card with the new word.
- Take out the cards once a day and study the new words.
- Add new words. Soon, you will have two piles of notecards: *Words I need to learn* and *Words I only need to review.*

razor

He shaves his face with a razor every morning.

Jobs 1

A Complete the sentences with the name of the correct job.

1. _____A construction worker_____ can build a house.

2. _____ repairs and maintains computers.

3. _____ cleans offices and buildings.

4. _____ publishes books and magazines.

5. _____ plans roads, bridges, and tunnels.

6. _____ puts together products in a factory.

7. _____ sews shirts, dresses, and other clothing.

8. _____ designs logos and advertising for companies.

B Write the name of the job next to each area of study.

1. engineering: _____an engineer_____

2. medicine: _____

3. computers: _____

4. drama: _____

5. architecture: _____

6. art: _____

7. accounting: _____

8. business: _____

9. dentistry: _____

C Write eight jobs that do not require a college education or a special license.

_____a delivery person_____   _____

_____   _____

_____   _____

_____   _____

D Read each advertisement from the telephone book. Write the name of the job.

ART PARNESS, _Accountant_
- Income tax returns
- New business planning
- Personal financial planning
  555-9872

KAPLIN BROTHERS, _____
- ❖ Indoor and outdoor lighting
- ❖ Air conditioning and ceiling fans
- ❖ Phone and cable wiring
  555-3248

JOHN ELBAUM, _____
- o Teeth whitening
- o Crowns and bridges
- o Full and partial dentures
  555-6672

CARMEN GARCIA, _____
- ✓ Creative haircuts
- ✓ Permanents and straightening
- ✓ Custom coloring
  555-4850

ANTON MICHAELS, _____
- Additions
- Custom home plans
- Complete planning and design
  555-6549

JONG HO PARK, _____
- ➤ Creative designs for weddings
- ➤ Funeral arrangements
- ➤ Cut flowers from around the world
  555-0945

CD 2
Track 22

E Listen to each speaker. Write the name of the correct job.

butcher	cashier	hairstylist	gardener
delivery person	~~architect~~	artist	babysitter

1. _____architect_____   5. _____

2. _____   6. _____

3. _____   7. _____

4. _____   8. _____

Word Work **Small Group**

Discuss the jobs in the dictionary. Complete the sentences.

1. _____ has a well-paid job.

2. _____ does the same thing over and over.

3. _____ is a blue-collar job.

4. _____ has good benefits.

5. _____ can run his/her own business.

Jobs 2

A **Complete the sentences with the name of the correct job.**

1. _____A pilot_____ flies a plane.

2. _____ plans vacations for clients.

3. _____ sells cars, furniture, or other items.

4. _____ takes pictures at weddings or other events.

5. _____ reports the news of important events.

6. _____ cares for sick or injured people.

7. _____ drives a taxi.

8. _____ checks people who walk into a building.

9. _____ defends clients in court.

10. _____ buys and sells stocks and bonds.

B **Complete the *Help Wanted* ads with the correct job.**

Wanted _____Reporter_____ to write news stories about local events. *Westwood Times.* 555-6783.	Licensed _____ to sell homes in the Westwood area. 555-1123.	**Full Time** _____ for both indoor and outdoor painting. Must have own transportation. Will train. 555-5937.
Sam's Service Center _____ to repair domestic and foreign cars. Exp. Req'd. 555-4309.	_____ for financial services company. Exp. with stocks and bonds, taxes, and financial planning. 555-0102.	Experienced _____ for second-grade class. Westwood Elementary School. 555-4000.
_____ to fly cargo planes on East Coast routes. Five years exp. 555-3761.	**Westwood Hospital** Part-time _____ to work in emergency room. Must be available weekends. 555-8100.	**Westwood Labs** _____ to work on research project. Must have strong chemistry background. 555-0304.
_____ to sell footwear at the Westwood Department Store. Evening hours. 555-0908.	_____ to work front desk at large law firm. Must speak English and have computer skills. 555-9000.	

C Write a good job for a person with each talent or interest.

1. A person who is good with numbers: _____a stockbroker_____

2. A person who loves animals: _____

3. A person who speaks well: _____

4. A person who enjoys performing for an audience: _____

5. A person who has good mechanical skills: _____

6. A person who enjoys traveling: _____

7. A person who likes children: _____

8. A person who is friendly and outgoing: _____

D Write eight jobs that a person can learn how to do on the job.

_____a security guard_____   _____

_____   _____

_____   _____

_____   _____

E Listen to each statement. Who is each person speaking to?

CD 2
Track 23

1. _____a receptionist_____   6. _____

2. _____   7. _____

3. _____   8. _____

4. _____   9. _____

5. _____   10. _____

Word Work Small Group

Discuss or write the answer to each question.

1. If you were a musician, what instrument would you like to play?
2. If you were a pilot, what country would you like to fly to?
3. If you were a taxi driver, what city would you like to drive in?
4. If you were a receptionist, what kind of office would you like to work in?
5. If you were a salesperson, what product would you like to sell?
6. If you were a high school teacher, what subject would you like to teach?

Working

A In your notebook, write about each person. What does each person do?

1.

2.

3.

4.

5.

6.

7.

8.

1. _____ This person designs houses. _____

B Complete the sentences.

1. A bus driver _____ drives _____ a bus.

2. A police officer _____ people who break the law.

3. A person with a fever _____ to work.

4. A personnel director _____ a new worker.

5. A babysitter _____ children.

6. A chef _____ creative dishes.

7. A secretary _____ letters on company letterhead.

8. A dentist _____ a patient's teeth.

9. An architect _____ homes and buildings.

10. A receptionist _____ a message for the boss.

Check the duties of an office assistant.

_____	1. To take messages		_____	7. To make copies
_____	2. To cook lunch for the boss		_____	8. To staple reports
_____	3. To open the mail		_____	9. To hire new salespeople
_____	4. To type letters and reports		_____	10. To use the computer
_____	5. To make company decisions		_____	11. To manufacture office supplies
_____	6. To call in sick		_____	12. To file papers and reports

CD 2
Track 24

D **Listen to each person. What is the person doing?**

1. _She's using a computer._

2. _____

3. _____

4. _____

5. _____

6. _____

7. _____

Word Work **Partners**

Read each sentence. Then, write another example for each verb.

1. File a letter.   _File a report._
2. Design a kitchen.   _Design a_
3. Manage a company.   _____
4. Repair a bicycle.   _____
5. Manufacture cameras. _____
6. Open the mail.   _____
7. Plan a wedding.   _____
8. Hire a painter.   _____

Farm

A Write the name of the baby animal.

1. _____a kid_____ 2. _____ 3. _____

4. _____ 5. _____ 6. _____

B Write the names of one or two farm animals.

1. Which animal can you ride?   __a donkey__   _____

2. Which animal gives wool?   _____

3. Which animal kills mice?   _____

4. Which animals are household pets?   _____   _____

5. Which animals lay eggs?   _____   _____

6. Which animals give milk?   _____   _____

7. Which animals provide food?   _____   _____

C Put the steps in order.

_____ **a.** Water the seeds.   __1__ **d.** Plow the field with the tractor.

_____ **b.** Plant corn seeds in the soil.   _____ **e.** Pick the corn.

_____ **c.** Put the corn in the silo.   _____ **f.** Watch the corn grow.

Complete the paragraph.

Mr. and Mrs. Jones are farmers. They live in a _____farmhouse_____. There is a
lot of work on the farm. Mr. Jones has four _____ to help him.
Mr. Jones gets up at 5:00 in the morning. He _____ the cows and
_____ the pigs and the horses. Mrs. Jones gets up early, too.
She gathers the eggs from the _____. Mr. Jones grows several
kinds of _____— corn, wheat, and alfalfa. He plows the
_____ in the spring with his _____. There is a
_____ in the field to keep the birds away. Every day, he checks
the apple trees in the _____ and the grapes in the
_____. In the fall, he _____ the apples from
the trees.

CD 2
Track 25

E **Look at each picture and listen to the statement. Circle *T* if the statement is
true. Circle *F* if the statement is false.**

1. T F	4. T F	7. T F	10. T F
2. T F	5. T F	8. T F	11. T F
3. T F	6. T F	9. T F	12. T F

Word Work **Partners**

Did you ever visit or live on a farm? List five things that you
did or that you saw.
  Examples: *I gathered the eggs. I rode on the tractor.*

Office

A Write the names of eight office items or people you see in the picture.

thumbtacks

_____   _____

_____   _____

_____   _____

_____   _____

B Look at the office in your dictionary. Write the location of each item.

1. Where is the business card file?   It's on the right side of the desk.

2. Where are the binders?   _____

3. Where is the tape?   _____

4. Where is the shredder?   _____

5. Where is the resume?   _____

6. Where is the pencil sharpener?   _____

7. Where is the photocopy?   _____

8. Where is the large file folder?   _____

9. Where is the fax machine?   _____

10. Where is the office manager?   _____

11. Where is the secretary?   _____

C Write the office manager's response to each request from the boss.

I'll put them in the shredder.	I'll get them from the supply cabinet.
I'll send it on the fax machine.	I'll get you her resume.
I'll look in your appointment book.	I'll make them on the copy machine.
~~I'll look in the file cabinet.~~	I'll get the calculator.

1. Where are the old sales reports? ___I'll look in the file cabinet.___

2. I need three copies of this report. _____

3. We don't need these reports anymore. _____

4. We need some more pencils. _____

5. When is the sales meeting? _____

6. I need to add these sales figures. _____

7. I'm interviewing Ms. Sims in five minutes. _____

8. The lawyer needs this letter immediately. _____

CD 2
Track 26

D Listen to each request. Write the number of the request next to the correct item or equipment.

_____ **a.** letterhead   _____ **e.** file cabinet

_____ **b.** calculator   _____ **f.** telephone

_____ **c.** pencil sharpener   _____ **g.** correction fluid

__1__ **d.** sticky note   _____ **h.** thumbtack

Word Work **Partners**

How is a company office today different from an office 100 years ago? Write eight office items that were not used in offices 100 years ago.

_____ _____

_____ _____

_____ _____

_____ _____

Factory

A Look at the picture of the factory in the dictionary. Circle *T* if the statement is true. Circle *F* if the statement is false.

1. There are four workers on the assembly line.   (T)   F

2. All the workers on the assembly line are wearing hairnets.   T   F

3. The machine operator is wearing safety earmuffs.   T   F

4. There are eight boxes on the forklift.   T   F

5. There's a truck at the loading dock.   T   F

6. A worker is loading boxes on the truck with a dolly.   T   F

7. The shipping clerk is wearing a hard hat.   T   F

B Put the steps for manufacturing baby strollers in order.

_____ **a.** Workers on the assembly line put on the seat, the safety belt, and the wheels.

__1__ **b.** Parts arrive at the factory.

_____ **c.** A robot tightens the wheels.

_____ **d.** At the end of the line, packers put the strollers into boxes.

_____ **e.** A forklift brings the packed boxes to the loading dock.

_____ **f.** A worker puts the stroller frames on the beginning of the conveyor belt.

C Match each hazard with an example.

__d__ **1.** biohazard   **a.** wires and cables

_____ **2.** electrical hazard   **b.** gasoline

_____ **3.** explosive materials   **c.** arsenic

_____ **4.** flammable materials   **d.** medical waste

_____ **5.** poisonous materials   **e.** uranium

_____ **6.** radioactive materials   **f.** dynamite

D Write the name of the safety equipment that protects each part of the body.

1. feet: _____safety boots_____

2. head: _____

3. eyes: _____   _____

4. lungs: _____   _____

5. ears: _____   _____

6. hair: _____

**CD 2
Track 27**

E Listen to each sentence and circle the letter(s) of the correct worker. If none of the workers is wearing the equipment, circle *None.*

	A				B				C				D

1. A   B   C   D   (None)   6. A   B   C   D   None

2. A   B   C   D   None   7. A   B   C   D   None

3. A   B   C   D   None   8. A   B   C   D   None

4. A   B   C   D   None   9. A   B   C   D   None

5. A   B   C   D   None   10. A   B   C   D   None

Word Work   **Small Group**

Write three rules for the factory in your dictionary.

Examples:

All workers must punch their time cards as soon as they report to work.

All workers must call the front office if they are going to miss a day of work.

Hotel

A **Complete the sentences.**

1. We have _____single rooms_____,

   _____, and large

   _____.

2. You can attend a meeting in one of our _____.

3. You can use the computers or make copies in our _____.

4. You can ask the _____ to get you tickets for a show.

5. You can buy souvenirs in our _____.

6. You can sit and relax in our _____.

7. You can celebrate a wedding or have a party in our _____.

8. You can exercise in our _____.

9. You can order dinner from our four-star _____.

B **Write the correct response.**

You can order from room service.	You can use the business center.
Call valet parking.	I'll call the bellhop.
In the ballroom.	You can speak with the concierge.
~~I'll call a housekeeper.~~	It's 11:00 a.m.

1. Our bed hasn't been made.   ____I'll call a housekeeper.____

2. We have four suitcases.   _____

3. I need to send a fax.   _____

4. We would like dinner in our room.   _____

5. Where is the art museum?   _____

6. What time is check-out?   _____

7. We need the car at 7:00 p.m.   _____

8. Where is the wedding reception?   _____

c **Complete the sentences about a terrible hotel stay.**

1. _____Room rates_____ were very high. We paid $250 a night.

2. The _____ at the registration desk was unfriendly.

3. We asked for a suite, but they only had _____.

4. The _____ was broken, and we had to walk up to the third floor.

5. The _____ didn't give us any towels.

6. _____ was very slow. We waited one hour for dinner.

7. There was no fax machine in the _____.

8. The children brought bathing suits, but the _____ was closed.

9. The _____ in the room next to ours partied until 2:00 a.m.

10. We had to get up early because the _____ time was 9:00 a.m.

CD 2
Track 28

D **Listen to the conversation between a desk clerk and a caller. Complete the information.**

1. The caller made a reservation for _____ nights.

2. She wants a (single room   double room   suite).

3. The room rate is _____ a night.

4. Check-in time is _____. Check-out time is _____.

5. The caller asked about the following features (fitness center   sauna

   business center   ballroom   gift shop   pool).

6. Parking is (free   an additional charge).

Word Work **Partners**

You are going to spend the weekend at a hotel in the city.
Rate these features from 1 (most important) to 8 (least
important). Discuss your choices with your partner.

_____ room rates   _____ business center

_____ free parking   _____ room service

_____ location   _____ concierge

_____ pool   _____ fitness center

Tools and Supplies 1

A Write the names of five tools in the tool belt.

_____pliers_____   _____

_____   _____

_____

B What tool is each person using?

1. ___a hammer___   2. _____   3. _____   4. _____

5. _____   6. _____   7. _____   8. _____

C Complete the sentences with one of the words in Exercise B.

1. Use _____a router_____ to make a decorative edge.

2. Use _____ to cut a piece of wood.

3. Use _____ to put in a nail in the wall.

4. Use _____ to make a small hole in a wall.

5. Use _____ to chop down a tree.

6. Use _____ to dig a hole.

7. Use _____ to make wood smooth.

8. Use _____ to tighten a pipe.

D Complete the questions.

1. Dig a hole.   Where's the _____?
2. Sand the wood.   Where's the _____?
3. Drill a hole.   Where's the _____?
4. Caulk the shower.   Where's the _____?
5. Break the rock.   Where's the _____?
6. Hold the wood tightly. Where's the _____?
7. Turn the screw.   Where's the _____?

CD 2
Track 29

E Listen and write the price under the correct item.

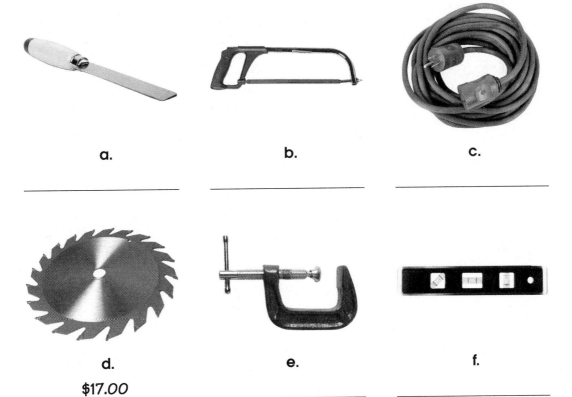

a.

b.

c.

_____   _____   _____

d.

e.

f.

$17.00

_____   _____   _____

Word Work **Partners**

You are going to buy tools for a small toolbox. Which six tools will you buy first?

_____   _____   _____

_____   _____   _____

Tools and Supplies 2

A **Complete the sentences.**

1. You put _____insulation_____ in the wall to keep a house warm.

2. You hammer a _____ into a wall.

3. You use a wrench to turn a _____.

4. You put _____ in a flashlight.

5. You turn a _____ with a screwdriver.

6. You build the frame of a house with _____.

7. You put _____ on a bathroom floor.

8. You hang a door on _____.

9. You hang a cup on a _____.

10. You sand wood with _____.

hinges
sandpaper
batteries
screw
~~insulation~~
hook
board lumber
tile
nut
nail

B **Complete the steps to paint a room.**

1. Fill any holes in the wall using spackle and a _____scraper_____.

2. Sand those areas with _____.

3. Tape the windows with _____.

4. Pour the paint into a _____.

5. Use a _____ to paint the ceiling and the walls.

6. Use a small _____ to paint the windows and molding.

C **Read the statements. Check *Good idea* or *Bad idea.***

	Good idea	Bad idea
1. Hang a mirror with duct tape.	____	✓
2. Put a padlock on a door.	____	____
3. Put molding around the edges of a room.	____	____
4. Put shingles on the ceiling.	____	____
5. Put a screw in an anchor.	____	____

D These workers are putting up drywall in a room. Write the tools and supplies that the workers need for each step.

1.
2.
3.
4.
5.
6.

1. Insulate the wall: _____ insulation _____

2. Measure and cut the drywall: _____

3. Put up the drywall: _____

4. Tape and spackle the seams: _____

5. Sand the seams: _____

6. Paint the walls: _____

CD 2
Track 30

E Listen to this order for a hardware store. Complete the list of items.

Quantity/Item

6 sheets of _____   2 rolls of _____

4 sheets of _____   4 door _____

2 boxes of _____   3 packages of _____

3 boxes of _____

Word Work | **Small Group**

Pretend you are going to build a bookcase. What tools and supplies do you need? Write out the steps you need to follow.

Drill, Sand, Paint

In your notebook, write a sentence about each picture. What is each worker doing?

1. 2. 3. 4.

5. 6. 7. 8.

1. _____ He is welding. _____

Complete the sentences. There are several correct answers.

1. If you want to ____ tear down a wall ____, you need a sledgehammer.

2. If you want to _____, you need a saw.

3. If you want to _____, you need a paintbrush.

4. If you want to _____, you need a shovel.

5. If you want to _____, you need a tape measure.

6. If you want to _____, you need a drill.

7. If you want to _____, you need a hammer.

8. If you want to _____, you need sandpaper.

9. If you want to _____, you need a pipe wrench.

CD 2
Track 31

C **Listen to the conversation between two friends. Answer the questions.**

1. Did the workers pour the concrete? (Yes) No

2. Did they dig a trench around the house? Yes No

3. Did they install the windows? Yes No

4. Did they put up the drywall? Yes No

5. Did they wire the house? Yes No

6. Did they cut and install the pipes? Yes No

7. Did they paint the house? Yes No

Word Work **Small Group**

Discuss or write the answers to the questions about building a house.

1. Which jobs require the most experience?
2. Which jobs require power tools?
3. Which jobs require a worker to measure carefully?

Word Study

Analyze your vocabulary study. For one week, record your study time and your study activities. How much time do you study vocabulary? What activities or methods are most effective for you? At the end of the week, have a class discussion. Different students can explain the activities that are helpful for them.

Example:

Day	Time	Activities
Monday	10 minutes	Vocabulary notecards
Tuesday	15 minutes	I studied the words on pages 158 and 159. I highlighted the words that were new for me and said them aloud.
Wednesday	15 minutes	Vocabulary notecards I wrote two new words in my vocabulary journal and wrote sentences with them.

Day	Time	Activities
Monday	_____	_____
Tuesday	_____	_____
Wednesday	_____	_____
Thursday	_____	_____
Friday	_____	_____
Saturday	_____	_____

Weather

A **Complete the sentences.**

1. A strong _____wind_____ blew the tree down.

2. A temperature of 10 degrees Celsius is approximately 50 degrees
   _____.

3. Sometimes there is a _____ in the sky after a rainstorm.

4. In a bad storm, _____ can hit a tree.

5. School was closed for a week because we had three feet of
   _____.

6. The lake is frozen. The _____ is ten inches thick.

7. It's raining lightly. I can see _____ on the window.

8. Look at those gray _____. It's going to rain.

9. The _____ shows that it is 30° outside.

10. The _____ were so big that they broke the windshield of my car.

11. Don't worry. It isn't going to snow because the temperature is above
    _____.

B **Write the missing word form. Then, complete the sentences with the correct form of the word.**

1. sun _____sunny_____ It's _____ today.

2. _____ rainy People use umbrellas on _____ days.

3. _____ stormy We're going to have a bad _____.

4. wind _____ It was so _____ that my hat blew off.

5. _____ cloudy There isn't a _____ in the sky.

6. _____ foggy It's difficult to drive in this _____.

7. _____ snowy The _____ is very deep.

8. _____ icy Don't slip on the _____.

C In your notebook, write about the weather conditions in these pictures. What do you think the temperature is? What are the people doing?

CD 3
Track 1

D Listen to the international weather report. Write the temperature and forecast for today and tomorrow for each country.

Country	Weather Today	Weather Tomorrow
Poland	very cold	heavy snow
Australia		
Japan		
Mexico		
Colombia		
France		

Word Work Partners

Some countries have four seasons. Other countries have two seasons. How many seasons do you have in your country? Describe the weather in each season. What is the average temperature for each season?

The Earth's Surface

A Write the word for each feature of the Earth's surface.

1. ___stream___

2. _____

3. _____

4. _____

5. _____

6. _____

7. _____

8. _____

B Complete the definitions.

1. ___A volcano___ is a mountain formed by hot, melted rock escaping from beneath the earth.

2. _____ is a piece of land completely surrounded by water.

3. _____ is water falling from a high place.

4. _____ is a body of water surrounded by land. The water is usually fresh.

5. _____ is an opening in the side of a mountain or cliff.

6. _____ is the area on both sides of a river.

7. _____ is a sandy area near a lake or ocean.

8. _____ is a river of ice.

9. _____ is a large body of salt water.

10. _____ is a long group of mountains.

11. _____ is an area that receives very little rain.

12. _____ is the highest part of a mountain.

C Write the names of nine features you see on this map.

_____peninsula_____   _____   _____

_____   _____   _____

_____   _____   _____

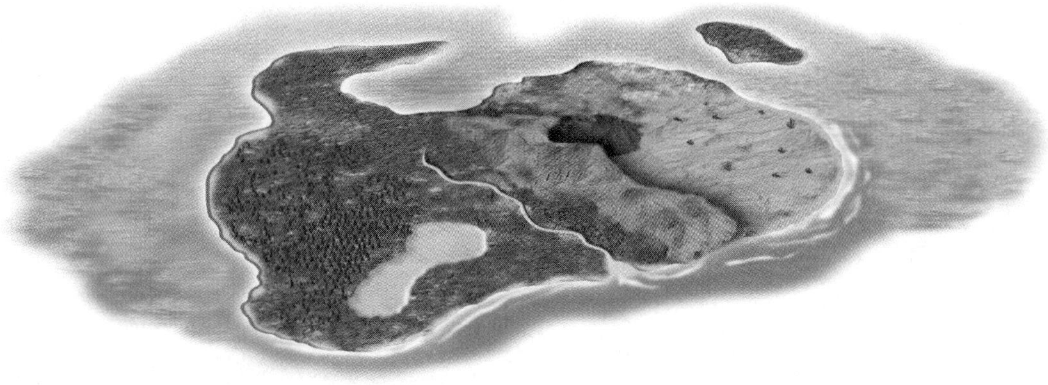

D Read the names of the places. Then, write the name of the feature.

Places	Feature
1. Sahara, Gobi, Patagonia	_____desert_____
2. Everest, K2, Denali	_____
3. Greenland, Borneo, Hawaii	_____
4. Andes, Himalayas, Rockies	_____
5. Amazon, Nile, Yangtze	_____
6. Pacific, Atlantic, Indian	_____

CD 3
Track 2

E Listen to the story of a long drive across the country. Write the nine features that are included in the story.

1. ____mountain range____   4. _____   7. _____

2. _____   5. _____   8. _____

3. _____   6. _____   9. _____

Word Work **Small Group**

What country do you live in?

Draw a map of the country or state you live in. Show the major geographic features, such as mountain ranges, lakes, rivers, deserts, and islands.

Energy, Pollution, and Natural Disasters

A Write the name of the type of energy in each picture.

1. <u>hydroelectric power</u>

2. _____

3. _____

4. _____

5. _____

6. _____

B Read each statement about the effects of pollution. Circle *T* if the statement is true. Circle *F* if the statement is false.

1. Water pollution contaminates drinking water. (T) F

2. Automobile exhaust kills fish. T F

3. Litter makes roads and cities look unattractive. T F

4. Pesticide poisoning can kill birds. T F

5. Air pollution destroys beaches. T F

6. Exposure to radiation can cause cancer. T F

7. An oil spill affects people's breathing. T F

C Read the descriptions of the natural disasters and complete the sentences.

1. Many people died during the ____<u>famine</u>____ because there wasn't enough food.

2. We had a bad _____ last winter. It snowed for three days. All the schools

   and businesses in our city closed.

3. There was a minor _____ in the city. The buildings shook, but none of them collapsed.

4. A large _____ hit the coast, killing all the people on the beach.

5. A _____ burned thousands of acres of trees.

6. The heavy rain caused a _____. People could only travel by boat.

7. An _____ raced down the mountain and covered the road with snow.

8. During the _____, people watched fire and smoke shoot out of the mountain. Hot lava flowed down the sides of the mountain.

D Write the names of five disasters that give people no warning. Write the names of five disasters that people know about a few hours or days before.

Disasters with no warning	Disasters with warning time
tornado	blizzard

E Listen to the three conversations. Write the number of the conversation under the correct picture.

a. _____ b. _____ c. _____

Word Work Small Group

Talk or write about a disaster that occurred in your country. What happened?

The United States and Canada

A **Write the capital city.**

1. The capital of the United States is _____Washington, D.C._____.

2. The capital of New York is _____.

3. The capital of California is _____.

4. The capital of Florida is _____.

5. The capital of Texas is _____.

6. The capital of Illinois is _____.

7. The capital of Canada is _____.

8. The capital of Quebec is _____.

9. The capital of Ontario is _____.

10. The capital of British Columbia is _____.

B **Read the description. Write the name of the state.**

1. This state is the largest state on the West Coast. _____California_____

2. This is one of the Rocky Mountain States. It shares a long border with Canada.

   _____

3. This is the largest state in the Southwest. _____

4. This state is in the South. It is on both the Atlantic Ocean and the Gulf of Mexico.

   _____

5. This state is a group of small islands in the Pacific Ocean. _____

6. This is the largest state in the United States. It borders British Columbia and the

   Yukon. _____

7. The smallest state in the United States is in New England. It borders Connecticut

   and Massachusetts. _____

8. This Midwest state is on the Mississippi River. It is between Kansas and Illinois.

   _____

C Write the names of the states or provinces you will drive through to reach each destination.

1. From Washington, D.C., to Florida: _____Virginia_____, _____,

_____, _____

2. From Sacramento, California, to Springfield, Illinois: _____Nevada_____,

_____, _____, _____

3. From Phoenix, Arizona, to Nashville, Tennessee: _____,

_____, _____, _____

_____

4. From Quebec City, Quebec, to Victoria, British Columbia: _____,

_____, _____, _____

CD 3
Track 4

D Listen to the information about the national parks. Write the name of the state where you find each park.

1. _____Colorado_____    2.  _____   3. _____

4.  _____   5.  _____   6. _____

Word Work | **Small Group**

Draw a state or a province. Add the bordering states, provinces, or territories one at a time. Who in the group can name the state or province first?

The World

A **Read each fact. Write the name of a continent or a country.**

1. _____Asia_____ is the largest continent.

2. _____ is a continent with no permanent residents.

3. _____ is a continent with only one country.

4. _____ is a large country in both Asia and Europe.

5. _____ is the largest country in South America in size.

6. _____ is a country in Europe with no seaport.

7. _____ is an island country in Asia.

8. _____ is a country on both the Atlantic and Pacific oceans.

9. _____ is the southernmost country in Africa.

B **These are the ten largest cities in the world in terms of population. Write the country for each city.**

India	Russia	Brazil	India	Turkey
Korea	Argentina	Philippines	~~China~~	Pakistan

1. Shanghai, ___China___

2. Mumbai (Bombay), _____

3. Buenos Aires, _____

4. Moscow, _____

5. Karachi, _____

6. Delhi, _____

7. Manila, _____

8. São Paolo, _____

9. Seoul, _____

10. Istanbul, _____

C **Read each statement. Circle *T* if the statement is true. Circle *F* if the statement is false.**

1. Africa is on the Equator.   (T)   F

2. The Equator divides the world into the Northern Hemisphere
   and the Southern Hemisphere.   T   F

3. The Northern Hemisphere is everything south of the Equator.   T   F

4. Australia is in the Northern Hemisphere.   T   F

5. Europe is in the Northern Hemisphere.   T   F

6. The North Pole is opposite the South Pole.   T   F

7. The South Pole is in the Antarctic Circle.   T   F

CD 3
Track 5

D **The population of the world is more than six billion people. The pie chart shows the percentage of the world's population that lives on each continent. Listen and write the name of the correct continent on each part of the chart.**

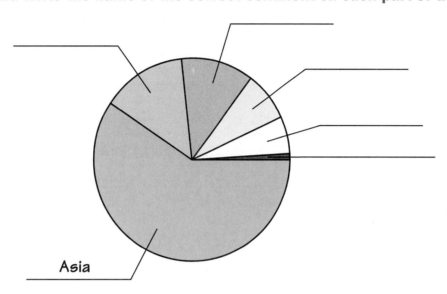

Asia

Word Work | **Small Group**

Look at the pictures. Name the country.

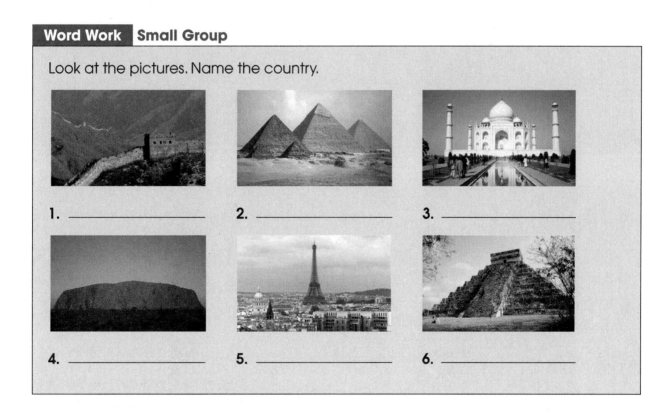

1. _____   2. _____   3. _____

4. _____   5. _____   6. _____

The Universe

A **Complete the information about the planets.**

There are nine planets in our solar system. The planets belong to two different groups. The four planets in the first group are small and rocky and are close to the sun. They are ___Mercury___, _____, _____, and _____. The four planets in the second group are made of gases and are far from the sun. They are _____, _____, _____, and _____. We know very little about the smallest and farthest planet, _____. It is so far from the sun that it is a frozen world.

B **Write the correct word.**

star	space	atmosphere	satellites
astronomers	moon	planets	space station
orbit	rocket	telescopes	~~sun~~

1. The largest body in our solar system is the ___sun___.

2. The _____ are very large, ball-shaped bodies that move around the sun. The movement around the sun is called an _____.

3. A _____ is a bright ball of hot gas in the sky. At night, it looks like a dot of light in the sky.

4. The _____ is the round natural object that orbits Earth.

5. The _____ is the air above Earth.

6. _____ is the area beyond Earth where the planets, stars, and moons are found.

7. _____ often work in an observatory. They look at the solar system through _____.

8. A _____ is a spacecraft in orbit around Earth in which astronauts can live and work for long periods of time. A _____ takes astronauts into space.

9. Weather _____ orbit Earth and send pictures and weather data from space.

CD 3
Track 6

C **Listen to the information about the universe. Then, circle *T* if the statement is true or *F* if the statement is false.**

1. The sun is a planet.   T   Ⓕ

2. The sun is made of gases.   T   F

3. Earth is the center of the universe.   T   F

4. All planets travel in the same orbit.   T   F

5. Earth is the first planet from the sun.   T   F

6. It takes 365 days for Earth to orbit the sun.   T   F

7. Every 24 hours Earth turns on its axis.   T   F

8. The area facing the sun has night.   T   F

9. The moon orbits Earth.   T   F

10. It takes one year for the moon to orbit Earth. T   F

Word Work Partners

A group of stars that looks like an animal or another object is called a constellation. In your dictionary, you can see the constellation called The Big Dipper. What other constellations do you know? Make a diagram of a constellation you know.

Word Study

Think of creative ways to write vocabulary words to help you remember their meanings. Here are three examples:

Garden

A Look at the picture of the garden in your dictionary. Write the color of each flower.

1. _____red_____ roses

2. _____ lilies

3. _____ marigolds

4. _____ geraniums

5. _____ daisies

6. _____ irises

7. _____ chrysanthemums

8. _____ daffodils

9. _____ violets

10. _____ sunflowers

B Write the names of five trees and five flowers.

Trees	Flowers
elm	daffodils

C Complete the sentences.

1. Most flowers grow from _____seeds_____.

2. Other flowers grow from _____. You plant them in the fall, and they come up the next spring or summer.

3. _____ go into the soil and bring water to the plant.

4. _____ is an example of an evergreen tree. It is green all year.

5. Many commercial flower growers start seeds in a _____.

6. Most trees have a strong central _____.

7. Many _____ grow from the trunk.

8. In the fall, _____ turn colors and fall from the trees.

9. In a pine tree, the seeds are found in the _____.

D **Put the steps in order.**

_____ The buds open and flowers fill the garden.

_____ The seed sends roots into the soil.

_____ Small buds grow on the stem.

_1_ A gardener plants the seeds.

_____ A small stem grows and leaves start to appear.

E **Write the name of the tree for each leaf or seed.**

pine tree   elm tree   maple tree   ~~oak tree~~

1. _oak tree_   2. _____   3. _____   4. _____

F **Listen to the description of each flower. Write the number of the flower under the correct picture.**

a.   b.   c.   d.   e.

_____   _____   _____   _____   _1_

Word Work	**Partners**

Discuss or write the answers to the questions.
1. Do you ever buy flowers for anyone? What is the occasion?
2. What kind of flowers do you sometimes buy for your house?
3. What flower would you like to receive for your birthday?
4. What flowers do women often carry when they get married?
5. Do you have a garden? What flowers do you grow?

Desert

A **Circle the correct answer.**

1. Which animal is more dangerous: (a scorpion) or a grasshopper?

2. Which animal can be poisonous: a snake or a moth?

3. Which insect has eight legs: a spider or a fly?

4. Which animal moves more slowly: a rat or a tortoise?

5. Which animal lives longer: a coyote or a tortoise?

6. Which insect can jump: an ant or a grasshopper?

7. Which animal can attack people: a mountain lion or a camel?

8. Which insect stings: a cricket or a scorpion?

B **Match the words and their definitions.**

___g___ 1. sand dune   **a.** a small rock

_____ 2. boulder   **b.** a place in the desert with water and trees

_____ 3. oasis   **c.** a tree with no branches and with large leaves at the top

_____ 4. palm tree   **d.** an area with little rain

_____ 5. desert   **e.** a large rock

_____ 6. pebble   **f.** a green desert plant that sometimes has needles

_____ 7. cactus   **g.** a hill of sand

C **Read each description. Write the name of the desert animal.**

| a camel | a mountain lion | an ant |
| a vulture | a lizard | ~~a coyote~~ |

1. This animal belongs to the dog family. It is the size of a medium-sized dog. It has a long nose, pointed ears, and a long tail. This animal is usually gray or tan. At night, it barks or cries very loudly. _____*a coyote*_____

2. This large animal walks slowly across the desert. It can go for many days without food or water. It lives off the fat that it stores in the hump on its back.

_____

3. This reptile has a long tail. It spends most of the day on warm rocks, waiting for insects to fly by. It catches the insects with its tongue. _____

4. This large bird is always looking for a free meal. It doesn't hunt. It flies for many hours, looking for dead animals to eat. _____

5. This common insect lives in a colony, where all the members work together. It can carry many times its weight. _____

6. This strong animal is part of the cat family. It hunts other animals. It often waits behind a boulder until a smaller animal is near. Then, it jumps out and attacks.

_____

CD 3
Track 8

D **Listen to each conversation between two people at a zoo. Then, read each statement and circle _T_ for true or _F_ for false.**

1.	Tortoises live in the water.	T	(F)
2.	Tortoises can grow to five feet long.	T	F
3.	Many animals attack tortoises.	T	F
4.	Tortoises eat insects such as scorpions and flies.	T	F
5.	Tortoises have strong teeth.	T	F
6.	There are more than 135 species of owls.	T	F
7.	Owls sleep at night.	T	F
8.	Owls eat insects and small birds.	T	F
9.	Owls move their eyes from side to side.	T	F
10.	Owls have ears.	T	F

Word Work **Partners**

Write a description of one of the animals in the desert. Don't write the name of the animal in your description. Read your description to the class. Can the other students guess the animal? (See Activity C for examples of how to write your descriptions.)

Rain Forest

A Try this crossword puzzle. Write the name of the animal.

Across

2

7

8

10

Down

1

3

4

5

6

9

B Write the words in the correct group.

~~chimpanzee~~	hummingbird	wasp	peacock	butterfly
aardvark	monkey	parakeet	alligator	beetle
caterpillar	flamingo	tarantula	gorilla	parrot

Animals	Birds	Insects
chimpanzee	_____	_____
_____	_____	_____
_____	_____	_____
_____	_____	_____
_____	_____	_____

C Look at the picture of the rain forest. Complete the sentences.

1. The ___monkey___ has a long tail. It's climbing a tree.

2. The _____ spends most of its life in trees. It's holding a vine.

3. The _____ is part of the cat family. It's orange with black stripes.

4. The _____ and the _____ spend most of the day swimming in the water or lying on a riverbank.

5. The _____ has a long nose. It can dig deep into the ground to find ants and other insects.

D Write the name of each bird or animal.

1. ___parakeet___   2. _____   3. _____

4. _____   5. _____   6. _____

E Listen to each statement. Write the name of the correct bird or animal from Exercise D.

CD 3
Track 9

1. ___parrot___   4. _____

2. _____   5. _____

3. _____   6. _____

Word Work **Partners**

Would you like to own a parrot or a parakeet? Write two advantages and two disadvantages to owning a pet bird.

Grasslands

A **Complete the paragraph.**

There are large areas of grasslands on most of the continents. Trees provide a home

for birds and insects, such as _____ sparrows _____ and _____.

Tall animals, such as _____, eat leaves from the taller trees. Some

animals, such as _____, spend most of the day in or near water

holes. The grass provides food for many animals. The tall grass hides some of the

smaller animals, such as _____ and _____. Some

animals, such as _____, live in tunnels under the ground.

B **Complete the sentences.**

1. _____ A giraffe _____ is very tall and has a long neck.

2. _____ has tusks and a long trunk.

3. _____ looks like a horse with stripes.

4. _____ has long antlers.

5. _____ has a mane and a long tail.

6. _____ has two short horns on its face.

7. _____ has two strong back legs and can hop long distances.

8. _____ has long fur and two horns on its head.

9. The hard foot of a mammal is _____. The soft foot of a mammal is

_____.

C **Read each statement. Circle *T* if the statement is true. Circle *F* if the statement is false.**

1. Hippopotami spend most of the day in the water.   (T)   F
2. Kangaroos are strong swimmers.   T   F
3. Ostriches can fly high above the grassland.   T   F
4. Elephants live in a group called a herd.   T   F
5. Elephants are the largest land animals.   T   F
6. Gophers live in trees.   T   F
7. Lions hunt other animals for food.   T   F
8. Lions runs faster than elephants.   T   F
9. Gazelles have long fur.   T   F
10. Antelope have tusks.   T   F

CD 3
Track 10

E **Listen to the information about five endangered animals. Check the reasons why the number of these animals is decreasing.**

Loss of habitat - The population of the world is growing. People need the land for homes and for growing food, so there is less land for animals.

Hunter - This is a person who looks for and kills animals for sport or for food.

Poacher – This is a person who hunts animals illegally.

	Loss of habitat	Hunters	Ranchers and farmers	Poachers
Rhinoceros	✓	_____	_____	✓
Elephant	_____	_____	_____	_____
Cheetah	_____	_____	_____	_____
Kangaroo	_____	_____	_____	_____
Zebra	_____	_____	_____	_____

Word Work **Partners**

Write five questions about animals that live in the grasslands.
Ask another group your questions.

Examples: **Which animal has two long legs and a long neck?**
Which animal has black and white stripes?

Polar Lands

A Complete the sentences with the name of the animal.

goose	~~polar bear~~	reindeer
penguin	falcon	whale

1. _____A polar bear_____ is one of the largest polar animals. It lives at sea half the time and on land the other half. It can walk up to forty miles a day.

2. _____ is a bird, but it cannot fly. It has flippers instead of wings. This animal lives in large groups, which can have 10,000 members or more.

3. _____ lives in the Arctic in the summer and then flies south for the winter.

4. _____ lives in the ocean, but it is not a fish. It is the largest mammal in the world. It must come to the surface to breathe air.

5. _____ has brown fur, but its neck and tail are white. It is a fast runner and an excellent swimmer. This animal lives in large herds of 1,000 or more.

6. _____ is the fastest bird in the world. It has very good eyes and can see food on the ground from a mile away.

B Complete the sentences. You will use some words more than once.

wings	beak	claws	tusks
flippers	antlers	whiskers	fur

1. An animal's _____whiskers_____ protect its face.

2. An animal uses its _____ to fly.

3. An animal's _____ protects it from the cold.

4. An animal can fight with its _____, its _____, its _____, or its _____.

5. A bird uses its _____ or _____ to hold things.

6. An animal uses its _____ to swim.

7. A bird uses its _____ to open, tear, and eat food.

C **Label the parts of each animal.**

tail	hoof		beak	feather	claw
fur	~~webbed feet~~		antlers	flipper	

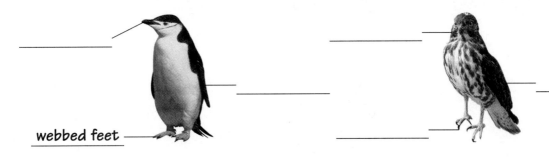

_____

webbed feet _____

_____

_____

_____

_____

_____

_____

CD 3
Track 11

D **Listen to descriptions of these four animals. Write the number of the description under the correct animal.**

a. ____   b. ____   c. ____   d. ____

Word Work   **Small Group**

Polar animals live in difficult conditions. It's cold most of the year in the Arctic. For many months, there is little or no sunlight. Snow covers the ground most of the year. How do polar bears survive in these conditions?

Sea

A Complete the sentences with the name of the animal.

1. ___crab___   2. _____   3. _____   4. _____

5. _____   6. _____   7. _____   8. _____

B Complete the sentences with the name of an animal from Exercise A.

1. ___A turtle___ spends most of its life in the water. Every two or three years, the female comes onto land and lays eggs.

2. With three rows of sharp teeth, _____ can be a dangerous fish. It eats other fish and sometimes even attacks people.

3. _____ lives near the beach. It can fly or land on the water. It catches small fish.

4. _____ has the shape of an umbrella. It lives near the surface of the water. Some of these animals can sting fish or people.

5. _____ has a flat body and a long tail. It can give a poisonous sting with its tail.

6. _____ is a mammal that comes to the surface every few minutes to breathe. This intelligent animal likes to jump and play.

7. _____ can be very small or as large as a dinner plate. It has eight legs and a hard shell. It can swim or walk on the beach.

C **Write the names of four more sea creatures in each group.**

A <u>vertebrate</u> is an animal with a backbone.

An <u>invertebrate</u> is an animal without bones. It has a soft body.

Vertebrates	Invertebrates
shark	octopus
tuna	sea anemone

CD 3
Track 12

D **The ocean is very deep. Listen and draw a line from each ocean creature to the depth at which it usually swims.**

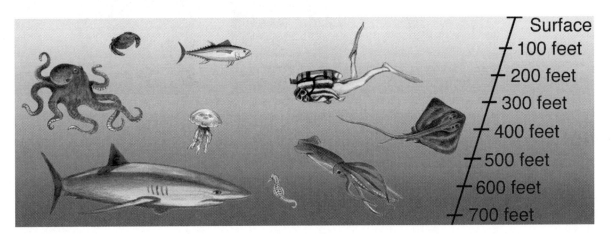

Surface
100 feet
200 feet
300 feet
400 feet
500 feet
600 feet
700 feet

Word Work **Small Group**

Discuss or write your answers.

1. You are a fisherman. Which fish would you like to catch?
2. You are a scuba diver. Which fish would you like to see?
3. You are a scientist. Which fish would you like to study?
4. You are a film director. Which fish would you like to make a documentary about?

Woodlands

A Write the name of each animal.

1. cardinal   2. _____   3. _____   4. _____

5. _____   6. _____   7. _____   8. _____

9. _____   10. _____   11. _____   12. _____

B Write the name of the correct woodland animal.

1. This long, thin animal is usually pink or gray. It lives in the ground. It is a favorite food for birds. ____worm____

2. This small animal has a furry tail. It can run up and down trees and jump from branch to branch. It collects nuts. _____

3. This bird has a long, sharp beak. It sits on a branch and makes holes in trees.

   _____

4. This large bird is the largest hunting bird. It uses its sharp claws to catch smaller animals. _____

5. This large woodland animal spends its day eating leaves, flowers, and fruit. The males grow antlers. _____

6. This animal lives in rivers and lakes. It can cut down trees with its strong front teeth. It builds its home, called a dam, in the water. _____

7. This animal walks slowly through the woods. The other animals do not bother it because sharp needles, called quills, cover its body. _____

8. This small animal is black with a white stripe on its back. When it thinks it is in danger, it gives off a terrible smell. _____

CD 3
Track 13

C **Listen to the description of each animal. Write the number of the description under the correct animal.**

a.	b.	c.	d.	e.

_____   _____   __1__   _____   _____

Word Work **Small Group**

Discuss or write the answers to these questions.

Which of these woodland animals live in your area?

Are any of these animals a problem in your area? Why?

Which of these animals will eat the vegetables in your garden?

Which of these animals live in the ground?

Which of these animals build nests in trees?

Word Study

Put vocabulary words into groups or categories. In this unit, you could classify animals several ways. For example:

1. Animals that run—Animals that swim—Animals that fly
2. Insects—Birds—Fish

Another way to classify words is to decide on one group and find several words that belong in that group, such as:

1. Animals that are dangerous
2. Animals that live in my country
3. Animals that are larger than I am

Math

A Write the names of two objects that are the same shape as each shape or solid.

circle	oval	rectangle	triangle
clock			

sphere	cube	cone	cylinder

B Complete the chart. Write the verb and the operation.

Sign	Verb	Operation	Example
+	add	addition	10 + 5 = 15
−	_____	_____	10 − 5 = 5
×	_____	_____	10 × 5 = 50
÷	_____	_____	10 ÷ 5 = 2

C Read the problem. Write the numbers and solve the problems.

1. Add 6 and 12. ___6 + 12 = 18___

2. Subtract 7 from 15. _____

3. Divide 20 by 5. _____

4. Multiply 3 by 5. _____

5. What is 5 times 6? _____

6. What is 20 minus 4? _____

7. What is 2 multiplied by 6? _____

8. What is 14 minus 4? _____

9. What is 10 plus 10? _____

D **Look at the math problems. Write each problem in words.**

1. $2 \times 8 = 16$ 2 times 8 equals 16.

2. $15 \div 3 = 5$ _____

3. $35 + 5 + 10 = 50$ _____

4. $25 - 5 = 20$ _____

5. $5 \times 5 = 25$ _____

E **Complete the sentences about each figure.**

1.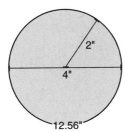

The _____radius_____ of the circle is 2".

The _____ is 4".

The _____ is 12.56".

2.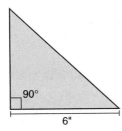

The _____ of the triangle is 6".

The _____ is 90°.

3.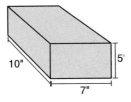

The _____ of the figure is 5".

The _____ is 7".

The _____ is 10".

CD 3
Track 14

F **Listen to each word problem. Write the numbers and solve the problem. What operation did you use?**

1. ____$.99 x 5 = $4.95____   Operation: ____multiplication____

2. _____ Operation: _____

3. _____ Operation: _____

4. _____ Operation: _____

5. _____ Operation: _____

Word Work **Small Group**

Write three math problems. Read each problem to your group. Your classmates will solve the problems.

Science

A **Match each picture with the correct description.**

1.

2.

3.

4.

5.

6.

___5___ **a.** The scientist is pouring liquid into a flask. He is using a funnel.

_____ **b.** The scientist is dropping liquid into a petri dish.

_____ **c.** The scientist is holding a beaker and a test tube.

_____ **d.** The scientist is looking into a microscope.

_____ **e.** The scientist is pouring liquid into a graduated cylinder. She is using a funnel.

_____ **f.** The scientist is pouring liquid from a beaker into a flask.

B **Complete the sentences.**

1. Use a ____funnel____ to help pour liquids into a flask.

2. Put a _____ on top of a flask.

3. Use a _____ to heat liquids or solids.

4. Use _____ to pick up small objects.

5. Use a _____ to examine small objects.

6. Put a _____ or a _____ under the microscope.

7. Use a _____ to separate light.

8. Use a _____ to pick up metal objects, such as iron and steel.

C Match the word and the definition.

_d_ 1. physics
___ 2. chemistry
___ 3. biology
___ 4. Bunsen burner
___ 5. flask
___ 6. test tube
___ 7. element
___ 8. atom
___ 9. balance
___ 10. prism

a. the science that studies elements, atoms, and molecules

b. a gas burner for heating chemicals

c. a thin glass tube used in science experiments

d. the science that studies energy and matter

e. the smallest unit of matter

f. the science that studies living things

g. a glass container with a long, narrow neck

h. a glass that separates light into colors

i. a basic chemical substance

j. a scale that compares the weight of two things

CD 3
Track 15

D Listen to the science lab instructions. Write the number of the statement under the correct picture.

a.
___

b.
___

c.
___

d.
___

e.
___

f.
___

g.
1

h.
___

Word Work **Small Group**

Draw three items you can find in a science lab. Your partners will try to guess the piece of equipment you drew.

Writing

A Complete the crossword puzzle.

Across

4 ,

6 m

7 I'll call you.

8 .

9 house

10 -

Down

1 ( )

2 :

3 ;

5 '

B Read the sentences. Correct the capitalization and add the missing punctuation. Then, complete the punctuation rules.

1. a dictionary gives the definitions of many words

   a. Begin the sentence with a _____*capital*_____ letter.

   b. Put a _____ at the end of the sentence.

2. The teacher said open your dictionaries.

   a. Put a _____ after the word *said*.

   b. Begin the word *open* with a _____ letter.

   c. Put _____ around the words of the teacher.

3. What kind of dictionary do you have

   a. Put a _____ at the end of the sentence.

4. Wonderful

   a. Put an _____ at the end of the sentence.

C Put the steps for writing an essay in the correct order.

_____ **a.** She wrote an outline with her best ideas.

_____ **b.** Yolanda brainstormed different ideas. She crossed out some of them.

_____ **c.** Yolanda showed the draft of her essay to two other students and got their feedback.

__1__ **d.** The teacher assigned the students an essay topic.

_____ **e.** Yolanda typed her essay.

_____ **f.** Yolanda wrote her first draft. She concentrated on her ideas and organization.

_____ **g.** Yolanda handed in her essay on the due date.

_____ **h.** Yolanda edited her essay. She made her ideas clearer, corrected grammar errors, and checked the punctuation.

D Listen and write the sentences you hear. Use the correct punctuation.

CD 3
Track 16

1. _What time is it?_____

2. _____

3. _____

4. _____

5. _____

6. _____

7. _____

Word Work **Partners**

With a partner, check the punctuation of the sentences you wrote in Exercise D. Label each punctuation mark you used.

Explore, Rule, Invent

A **Write the verb for each person.**

Person	Verb
1. explorer	_explore_
2. inventor	
3. winner	
4. composer	
5. ruler	
6. builder	
7. migrant	
8. grower	
9. sailor	
10. producer	

B **Complete the sentences.**

1. A company _introduces_ a faster, smaller computer.

2. A spaceship _____ the moon.

3. Astronauts _____ the surface of the moon.

4. Soldiers _____ a country.

5. Citizens _____ a president.

6. A scientist _____ a cure for a disease.

7. Workers _____ a bridge across a river.

8. A jet _____ around the world.

9. A boat _____ across the ocean.

10. Soldiers can go home when a war _____.

11. A dictator _____ a country.

12. A factory _____ electronic equipment.

defend
build
~~introduces~~
ends
reaches
discovers
flies
explore
rules
sails
produces
elect

C **Match the person, country, or company and the achievement.**

_e_ 1. Ferdinand Magellan

_____ 2. Charles Lindbergh

_____ 3. Karl Benz

_____ 4. Galileo Galilei

_____ 5. Marie Curie

_____ 6. Russia

_____ 7. The Chunnel

_____ 8. Wolfgang Amadeus Mozart

_____ 9. Mao Zedong

_____ 10. Mother Teresa

a. builds the first automobile.

b. composes *Don Giovanni* and *The Magic Flute.*

c. flies solo across the Atlantic Ocean.

d. rules China for more than 25 years.

e. sails around the world.

f. wins the Nobel Peace Prize.

g. launches the first space station.

h. discovers radium.

i. opens between England and France in 1994.

j. invents the telescope.

CD 3
Track 17

D **Listen to the description of each event. Write the number of the description under the correct picture.**

a. _____

b. _____

c. _____

d. _1_

e. _____

f. _____

g. _____

h. _____

Word Work **Small Group**

As a group, list five important inventions. Try to put them in order. Which item was invented first, second, third, etc.?

U.S. Government and Citizenship

A **Name these past presidents of the United States.**

| George H. W. Bush | Ronald Reagan | Bill Clinton | ~~Jimmy Carter~~ |

1. _____Carter_____   2. _____   3. _____   4. _____

B **A person who wants to become a citizen of the United States must pass a citizenship test. Match the questions and answers.**

__c__ **1.** What are the colors of the flag?

_____ **2.** How many stars are on the flag?

_____ **3.** What does each star mean?

_____ **4.** When is Independence Day celebrated?

_____ **5.** What are the two major political parties?

_____ **6.** In what month do citizens vote for president?

_____ **7.** Who becomes president if the president dies?

_____ **8.** Where does the president live?

_____ **9.** Who elects the Congress?

a. one is for each state

b. July 4th

c. red, white, and blue

d. in the White House

e. Democrats and Republicans

f. fifty

g. the people

h. November

i. the vice president

C **Complete the sentences about the U.S. government.**

The _____Constitution_____ is the document that created the government of the United States. The government of the United States has three branches: the legislative branch, the executive branch, and the judicial branch. The legislative branch is called _____. The legislative branch makes the laws.

It includes two parts, the House of Representatives and the _____.

The 435 members of the House of Representatives are called _____.

The 100 members of the Senate are called _____. The executive

branch is the president and the _____. People

_____ for a president every four years. All _____

can vote. The executive branch is responsible for carrying out the laws. The

_____ is the judicial branch. The judicial branch interprets the laws.

There are nine _____ on the Supreme Court.

CD 3
Track 18

D **Listen to each question and answer. Then, check *Citizen, Permanent Resident,* or both.**

citizen—a person who was born in the United States or who has become a naturalized citizen

permanent resident—a person who was born in another country and who applied to live permanently in the United States

	Citizen	Permanent Resident
1. Does everyone have to obey the law?	✓	✓
2. Can everyone vote for president?	____	____
3. Does everyone have to pay taxes?	____	____
4. Can everyone serve on a jury?	____	____
5. Can everyone protest?	____	____
6. Can everyone serve in the military?	____	____

Word Study

One of the best ways to remember vocabulary words is to write sentences using the words. Write sentences that are true and that relate to your life.

Examples:

The president of my country is _____.

Scientists are trying to discover a cure for cancer.

The periodic table is on the wall in my chemistry class.

Fine Arts

A Complete the forms of each word.

Verb	Artist	Product
paint	painter	_____
sculpt	_____	_____
	potter	_____
photograph	_____	_____

B Write the names of two kinds of equipment or materials that each artist uses.

1. photographer: _____camera_____   _____

2. painter: _____   _____

3. potter: _____   _____

4. sculptor: _____   _____

C Complete the sentences.

1. A _____portrait_____ is a painting of a person.

2. A _____ is a painting of an outdoor scene.

3. A _____ is a painting of a group of objects, often fruit, flowers, or table items.

4. A _____ is a large painting that covers a wall.

5. An artist will often make a _____ of a scene before painting it.

6. Before painting, an artist puts the paint on a _____.

7. An artist sets the canvas on an _____.

8. A person who sits for a painting is a _____.

9. An artist uses a _____ to paint on a canvas.

10. People put a _____ around the edges of a completed painting or photograph.

D Write the correct response to each question.

> He's a sculptor.
>
> ~~I like modern art.~~
>
> It's a vase of flowers.
>
> It's on the side of the building.
>
> It's the countryside in the winter.
>
> That's my daughter.
>
> He uses clay.
>
> He uses oil paint.

1. What kind of art do you like? ___I like modern art.___

2. What kind of paint does he use? _____

3. What kind of artist is he? _____

4. What material does he use? _____

5. What is that a still life of? _____

6. What is that a landscape of? _____

7. Who is that a portrait of? _____

8. Where is the mural? _____

CD 3
Track 19

E Listen to the four conversations in a museum. Write the type of art that each visitor wants to see. Then, write the name of the correct section of the museum.

	Art	Section
1.	modern art	C
2.		
3.		
4.		

Word Work Small Group

Discuss each painting. Do you like the style and the colors? Why or why not?

Performing Arts

A **Complete the definitions.**

1. _____A dancer_____ is a person who dances.

2. _____ is a person who plays the drums.

3. _____ is a person who shows people to their seats in a theater.

4. _____ is a person who acts in a movie or play.

5. _____ is a person who conducts an orchestra.

6. _____ is a person who sings.

7. _____ is a person who plays the guitar.

8. The _____ watches a performance and applauds at the end of the show.

B **Write one type of performance for each performer.**

1. dancers: _____ballet_____

2. actors: _____

3. singers: _____

4. singers and backup singers: _____

5. musicians and conductor: _____

C **Read the statement. Circle *T* if the statement is true. Circle *F* if the statement is false.**

1. You buy tickets at the box office. (T) F

2. Actors usually perform on a stage. T F

3. The conductor leads the orchestra. T F

4. After a performance, the audience bows. T F

5. In an opera, the performers sing. T F

6. At a rock concert, there are spotlights on the singers. T F

7. The backup singers stand at the front of the stage. T F

D **Complete the information.**

Would you like to see a symphony orchestra? First, buy your _____ **tickets** _____ at the box office. On the day of the performance, arrive at the _____

early. The usher will give you a _____ and then show you to your

_____. You will see the orchestra on the _____.

When the _____ enters, the _____ will applaud.

The conductor will signal for silence. Then, the _____ will begin to

play. There is often a solo by a well-known _____. When the concert

is over, the audience will _____. The conductor and musicians will

_____.

CD 3
Track 20

E **Listen to each speaker talk about a performance he or she attended. Write the number of the conversation next to the correct performance.**

_____ **a.** ballet

_____ **b.** rock concert

_____ **c.** symphony orchestra

_____ **d.** play

Word Work **Small Group**

Write the name of a popular performer or group.

Rock group: _____

Singer: _____

Actor: _____ Actress: _____

Dancer: _____

Symphony orchestra: _____

Instruments

A Write the name of the instrument each person is playing.

1. _____trumpet_____ 2. _____ 3. _____

4. _____ 5. _____ 6. _____

B Write the name of the two instruments that are found in each section of an orchestra.

1. the brass section: _____trombone_____ _____

2. the string section: _____ _____

3. the percussion section: _____ _____

4. the keyboard section: _____ _____

5. the woodwind section: _____ _____

C Listen and write the name of the instrument you hear.

CD 3
Track 21

1. _____a harmonica_____ 6. _____

2. _____ 7. _____

3. _____ 8. _____

4. _____ 9. _____

5. _____ 10. _____

D **Look at the drawing of the symphony orchestra below. Complete the paragraph with the names of the instruments.**

The conductor is standing in front of the symphony orchestra. To his left and in front

of him, there are ten _____violins_____. There are four _____

to his right. Behind the cellos, there is one _____.

This orchestra has four types of woodwind instruments. There are three

_____, two _____, two _____,

and one _____.

The brass section is behind the woodwind section. There are six brass instruments

in this orchestra. On the left, there are two _____ and two

_____. There is one _____ and one

_____.

The percussion instruments are in the back. The _____ and

_____ are behind the other instruments. There is also a

_____.

Film, TV, and Music

A Write the word for each kind of movie or TV show.

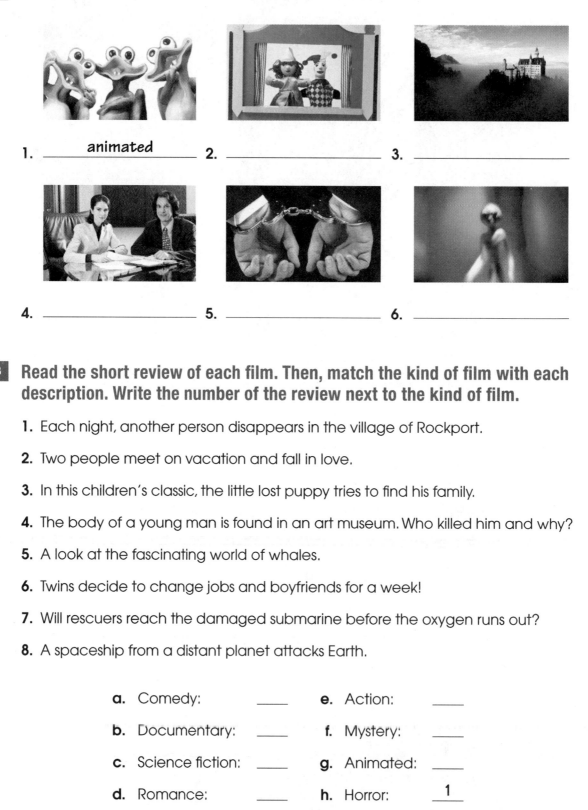

1. _____animated_____   2. _____   3. _____

4. _____   5. _____   6. _____

B Read the short review of each film. Then, match the kind of film with each description. Write the number of the review next to the kind of film.

1. Each night, another person disappears in the village of Rockport.

2. Two people meet on vacation and fall in love.

3. In this children's classic, the little lost puppy tries to find his family.

4. The body of a young man is found in an art museum. Who killed him and why?

5. A look at the fascinating world of whales.

6. Twins decide to change jobs and boyfriends for a week!

7. Will rescuers reach the damaged submarine before the oxygen runs out?

8. A spaceship from a distant planet attacks Earth.

    a. Comedy: _____   **e.** Action: _____

    b. Documentary: _____   **f.** Mystery: _____

    c. Science fiction: _____   **g.** Animated: _____

    d. Romance: _____   **h.** Horror: __1__

C **Write the type of film or TV program you can associate with these words.**

1. funny, laugh: _____ comedy _____

2. detective, crime: _____

3. score, baseball: _____

4. bulletin, update: _____

5. love, boyfriend: _____

6. prize, contestants: _____

7. cowboys, Indians: _____

8. scary, monster: _____

CD 3
Track 22

D **Listen to these lines from TV programs. On which type of TV program will you hear these lines?**

_____ **a.** children's program   __1__ **d.** news

_____ **b.** game show   _____ **e.** nature program

_____ **c.** soap opera   _____ **f.** talk show

Word Work **Small Group**

Discuss or write your answers to these questions about music.
1. What kind of music do you enjoy?
2. Who is your favorite singer?
3. What is your favorite group?

Word Study

Use other sources to help you learn and practice vocabulary words.

If you have the dictionary or the workbook CDs, listen to them at home. Repeat the words and sentences.

If you have access to the Internet, visit the websites of museums and read about a famous artist in English.

If you enjoy music, buy a CD of your favorite music with English lyrics.

If you live in an English-speaking country, read the TV guide of a newspaper in English.

Beach

A Complete the advertisement about this beach resort. Circle the correct word.

Enjoy a week in the sun at beautiful Laguna Beach Resort.

1. ((Swim)   Wave) in one of our three pools.

2. Walk on one of our beautiful (fins   sand) beaches.

3. Open a book and relax in one of our comfortable (beach chairs   snorkels).

4. Fish from our ocean (pier   life jacket).

5. Rent one of our many (sailboats   swimmers).

6. Take a (shovel   surfing) lesson.

7. Your children will enjoy the Kids Program. There is a (sand castle   water wing) building contest, a (seashell   cooler) hunt, and (lighthouse   beach ball) games. There is always a (sunbather   lifeguard) on duty to watch the children in the water.

8. Put on a mask and (snorkel   shovel) to explore life under the sea.

B Complete the chart. Write the person who performs each action.

1. sunbathe ___ sunbather ___

2. water-ski ___

3. swim ___

4. dive ___

5. sailboard ___

6. surf ___

7. snorkel ___

C Complete the sentences.

1. _____ pulls a water-skier.

2. _____ shows ships that they are near a dangerous area.

3. The surfers are happy today because the _____ are big.

4. It's very sunny. _____ sunscreen on your face and back.

5. My children can't swim well, so they wear _____.

6. You can breathe and see underwater if you wear a _____

   and a _____.

D In your notebook, write about each picture. What is each person doing?

1.

2.

3.

4.

5.

6.

1. ___A man is diving into the water._____

CD 3
Track 23

E Listen. Check the items that this family is bringing to the beach.

✓ surfboard	___ beach ball	___ towels
___ cooler	___ sunscreen	___ snorkel
___ water wings	___ umbrella	___ fins
___ pail and shovel	___ beach chairs	___ mask

Word Work **Partners**

You are going to stay at a beach resort for five days. Write five sentences about what you plan to do.

Camping

A Who uses each piece of equipment? Write the name of the correct person under each picture.

1. _____a rock climber_____   2. _____   3. _____

4. _____   5. _____   6. _____

B Complete the sentences about a bad camping trip. What equipment did the camper forget?

1. _____I forgot the matches_____, so I couldn't light the campfire.

2. _____, so I couldn't go fishing.

3. _____, so the mosquitoes bit me all day.

4. _____, so I couldn't see in the dark.

5. _____, so I couldn't cook dinner.

6. _____, so I had to sleep on the hard ground.

7. _____, so I got lost!

8. _____, so I couldn't use the canoe.

9. _____, so I was thirsty on my hike.

10. _____, so I couldn't go rock climbing.

C **Complete the story of this camping trip.**

My friends and I took a ten-day trip along the Colorado River through the Grand Canyon. We traveled in (rafts   tents). At times, the river was calm. Other times, we had to use our (compasses   paddles) to control the raft. We (camped   drove) next to the river. It only took a few minutes to set up our (tents   ropes). In the afternoons, some people (hiked   swam) in the river. Other people hiked up different (maps   trails). At night, we cooked our food on a (camping stove   lantern). After dinner, we sat around the (canoe   campfire) and talked. Sleeping was very comfortable because we had both (fishing poles   air mattresses) and (sleeping bags   canteens).

CD 3
Track 24

D **Listen as a man and a woman pack their backpacks for a camping trip. Circle who will carry each piece of equipment, the man (*M*), the woman (*W*), or both.**

1. camping stove	(M)	W	7. fishing pole	M	W
2. matches	M	W	8. sleeping bag	M	W
3. food	M	W	9. air mattress	M	W
4. trail map	M	W	10. tent	M	W
5. pocket knife	M	W	11. canteen	M	W
6. compass	M	W	12. insect repellent	M	W

Word Work | **Small Group**

Discuss or write about different locations in your area.
1. I can camp at _____.
2. I can hike in _____.
3. I can rent a canoe or raft at _____.
4. I can fish in _____.

City Park

A **Complete the words.**

1. monkey _____**bars**_____   5. jungle _____

2. _____ show   6. amusement _____

3. _____ can   7. _____ basket

4. roller _____   8. street _____

B **Look at the picture. Complete the sentences about the park.**

1. Two children are climbing on the _____**jungle gym**_____.

2. Someone is buying hot dogs from the _____.

3. A family is having a _____.

4. Several children are riding the horses on the _____.

5. Some children are watching the _____.

6. A boy is flying his _____.

7. A little boy is playing in the _____ while his mother is reading.

8. A boy is going down the _____.

9. A boy is putting his paper in the _____.

C **Write the correct verb. You can use a verb more than once.**

fly	watch	ride	climb	walk	sit

1. _____**ride**_____ a carousel   7. _____ at a picnic table

2. _____ on the jungle gym   8. _____ on the path

3. _____ a bicycle   9. _____ a Ferris wheel

4. _____ a puppet show   10. _____ a kite

5. _____ across the bridge   11. _____ in the sandbox

6. _____ on the monkey bars   12. _____ a roller coaster

D Write the correct answer from the box.

Yes. It's a windy day.	~~Let's stop at the street vendor.~~
She's on the swings.	I made chicken sandwiches.
I'll go on it with you.	She fell off the monkey bars.
On the path.	In the trash can.

1. I'm hungry.   <u>Let's stop at the street vendor.</u>

2. Mom, can I fly my kite?   _____

3. Where should I put the garbage?   _____

4. Where is she jogging?   _____

5. How did she break her leg?   _____

6. I'm scared of the roller coaster.   _____

7. Where is your daughter?   _____

8. What's in the picnic basket?   _____

CD 3
Track 25

E Listen to each statement. Write the number of the statement under the correct picture.

____   ____   1   ____

____   ____   ____   ____

Word Work | **Partners**

Plan a local park for your area. Include a small pond, paths, a playground with equipment, and a picnic area. What other things will you include? Draw a map of your park and label each item.

Places to Visit

A Write the name of each place to visit.

1. __bowling alley__ 2. _____ 3. _____ 4. _____

5. _____ 6. _____ 7. _____ 8. _____

B Write the names of four places that you can visit for free. Write four places that you have to pay admission.

These places are free:

_____**hiking trail**_____

_____

_____

_____

You have to pay admission:

_____

_____

_____

_____

C Complete the sentences.

1. If you are looking for a bargain, stop at several _____**garage sales**_____.

2. If you want to buy flowers for your garden, go to a _____.

3. If you enjoy animals, go to a _____.

4. If you want to learn more about the solar system, visit a _____.

5. If you have children and it's a hot day, cool off at a _____.

6. If you are hungry, stop at a _____.

7. If you are a sports fan, get tickets to a _____.

8. If you want to see that film, it's playing at the _____ in town.

D Read each statement. Check *Possible* or *Not possible.*

	Possible	Not possible
1. You can see lions at an aquarium.	___	✓
2. You can ride the roller coaster at a nursery.	___	___
3. You can watch a sporting event at a stadium.	___	___
4. You can play pool at a museum.	___	___
5. You can touch the animals at a petting zoo.	___	___
6. You can lift weights at a rodeo.	___	___
7. You can watch the elephants at a circus.	___	___
8. You can use a computer at an Internet café.	___	___
9. You can swim in the pool at a water park.	___	___
10. You can buy plants at a video arcade.	___	___

CD 3
Track 26

E Listen to each speaker. Write the number of each statement next to the correct location.

___ **a.** amusement park   ___ **e.** circus

___ **b.** miniature golf course   ___ **f.** hiking trail

___ **c.** planetarium   ___ **g.** art museum

_1_ **d.** bowling alley   ___ **h.** aquarium

Word Work Small Group

Choose four places to visit. Write the name of a specific place in your area.

Kind of Place:	Specific Place in My Area:
museum	The Museum of Modern Art
_____	_____
_____	_____
_____	_____

Indoor Sports and Fitness

A Write the name of the sport for each piece of equipment.

1. _____   2. _____   3. _____

4. _____   5. _____   6. _____

B Complete the chart.

Sport	Athlete	Place
basketball	basketball player	basketball court
_____	ping-pong player	ping-pong table
_____	boxer	_____
_____	_____	wrestling mat
_____	gymnast	gym
weightlifting	_____	gym
diving	_____	_____

C **Complete the sentences.**

In our area there is a popular gym with many members. It's busy all day.

In the exercise room, people ride the ___stationary bikes___ or run on the

_____. Some people sit on the mats and do exercises, such as

_____ or _____. In the weight room, weightlifters

lie on _____ and lift weights. There is a large gym where the local

_____ team practices. In our area, _____

is the most popular sport and there is a room with twenty tables! In the

_____ class, people exercise to music. Lots of people relax in the

_____ classes. The _____ classes are always full

and many of the people have earned black belts. The newest addition is an

Olympic-size _____ with eight swimming lanes. After they exercise,

members can shower and change in the men's or women's _____.

CD 3
Track 27

D **Listen to the information about each person's exercise routine. First, write the number of each speaker under the correct picture. Then, write the two indoor sports or fitness activities each person participates in.**

____   _1_   ____

_____   basketball   _____

_____   _____   _____

Word Work | **Partners**

Imagine that you are going to join a gym. You will use the gym at least three days a week. List the days. Then, plan your exercise schedule. Describe your exercise schedule to a partner.

Outdoor Sports and Fitness

A Write the name of the sport for each piece of equipment.

1. _____baseball_____   2. _____   3. _____

4. _____   5. _____   6. _____

B Complete the sentences with the name of a sports item from Exercise A.

1. In football, a player wears a _____ to protect his head.

2. In volleyball, players hit the ball over a _____.

3. Players can kick or head a _____.

4. In baseball, a player hits the ball with a _____bat_____.

5. In tennis, a player hits the ball with a _____.

6. In golf, a player hits the ball with a _____.

C Write three individual sports and three team sports.

Individual Sports	Team Sports
tennis	

D Read each statement. Circle *T* if the statement is true. Circle *F* if the statement is false.

1. In baseball, players hit the ball with a club.   T   (F)

2. A baseball player wears a uniform.   T   F

3. A baseball player catches the ball in a glove.   T   F

4. Soccer is played on a soccer field.   T   F

5. Many fans attend soccer games.   T   F

6. Soccer players wear helmets.   T   F

7. People play tennis on a golf course.   T   F

8. Tennis players hit the ball over a net.   T   F

9. Volleyball players can kick the ball.   T   F

10. In volleyball, players try to hit the ball through the goalposts.   T   F

CD 3
Track 28

E Listen to each statement. Write the number of the statement next to the correct sport.

____ **a.** baseball

____ **b.** track

____ **c.** football

_1_ **d.** soccer

____ **e.** golf

____ **f.** volleyball

____ **g.** tennis

Word Work	Small Group

Discuss each sports team. How many players are on a team?

Soccer ____   Rugby ____

Baseball ____   Football ____

Volleyball ____   Basketball ____

Choose one sport. Write three rules of the game.

Winter Sports

A **Complete the chart.**

Sport	Athlete	Equipment
ice skating	_ice skater_	_____
_____	hockey player	_____
_____	skier	_____
_____	cross-country skier	skis
_____	_____	snowboard

B **Write the athlete who wears this equipment.**

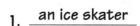

1. _an ice skater_   2. _____   3. _____   4. _____

C **Look at the picture of the hockey game. Complete the sentences.**

1. _____Ice hockey_____ is a popular winter sport.

2. There are six _____ on each team.

3. The game is played on an _____.

4. The players wear _____ on their feet.

5. They try to hit a _____ with their _____.

6. When they get the puck in the _____, they score one point.

7. The fans can look at the _____ to see the score.

D In your notebook, write about each picture. Where are the people? Write about their activities, equipment, and clothing.

1.

2.

3.

4.

CD 3
Track 29

E Listen to the information about each winter sport. Is the sport part of the winter Olympic games? Circle *Yes* or *No*.

1. ice skating — (Yes)   No

2. snowshoeing — Yes   No

3. downhill skiing — Yes   No

4. cross-country skiing — Yes   No

5. tobogganing — Yes   No

6. ice hockey — Yes   No

7. snowboarding — Yes   No

Word Work   **Small Group**

Discuss or write the answers to the questions.
1. Which winter sports have you tried?
2. What equipment did you need? What did you wear?
3. Which sports look easy? Which sports look difficult?
4. Do you like to watch winter sports? Which sports do you like to watch?
5. When and where are the next Winter Olympics?

Games, Toys, and Hobbies

A Write the name of the game or activity under each item.

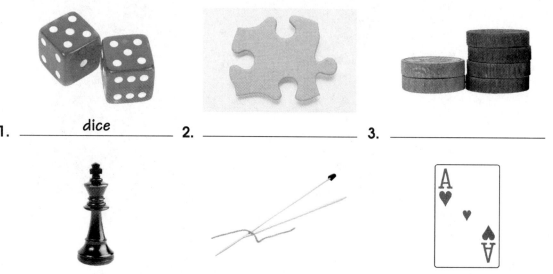

1. _____dice_____   2. _____   3. _____

4. _____   5. _____   6. _____

B Complete the sentences about the games and activities you know how to play or know how to do.

I know how to   I don't know how to

1. _____ play chess.
2. _____ play dominoes.
3. _____ crochet.
4. _____ knit.
5. _____ embroider.
6. _____ build a model.

C Complete the sentences.

1. Chess and checkers are two ____board games____.

2. In checkers, the _____ are black and red.

3. There are 52 cards in a _____.

4. In order to knit, you need _____ and _____ .

5. My son likes to build _____ of planes and ships.

6. Can you put together a _____ with 500 pieces?

7. Children like to color with _____ .

8. Bridge is a popular _____ game.

D In your notebook, write about the pictures. What are the people doing? Describe the game or activity.

1.
2.
3.

4.
5.
6.

CD 3
Track 30

E Listen. Write the number of the card you hear under the correct picture.

a.   b.   c.   d.   e.   f.   g.

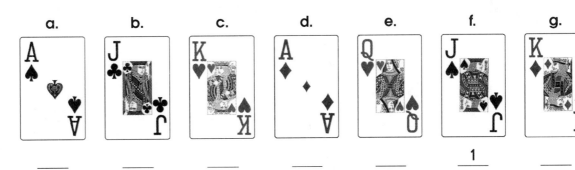

_____   _____   _____   _____   _____   1   _____

Word Work   **Small Group**

Bring a deck of cards to class. Teach the students in your group a card game from your country.

Camera, Stereo, and DVD

A **Complete the sentences. What kind of equipment do you use?**

1. _You use a satellite dish_ to get good reception.

2. _____ to keep a camera steady.

3. _____ to take photographs.

4. _____ to play video games.

5. _____ to take pictures of people that are far away.

6. _____ to record a child's birthday party.

7. _____ to change channels.

B **Put the steps in order to listen to a music CD.**

____ Insert the CD into the CD player.

____ Press *Play.*

_1_ Choose a CD.

____ Eject the disk.

____ Listen to the music.

C **Match the statement and the response.**

_c_ 1. I can't study when you're listening to a CD.

____ 2. I'll take some pictures at the party..

____ 3. That music is too loud.

____ 4. I can't plug the TV in.

____ 5. Do you have the remote control?

____ 6. The music is too low. I can't hear it.

____ 7. How can I listen to this cassette?

a. I'll turn it up.

b. You need an adapter.

c. I'll put my headphones on.

d. Yes. What channel do you want?

e. Use the stereo.

f. I'll turn it down.

g. Don't forget your camera.

D In your notebook, write a few sentences about each picture. What equipment is each person using? What is he/she doing?

1.

2.

3.

4.

5.

6.

CD 3
Track 31

E Listen to each statement. Circle the correct response.

1. **a.** I'll pause it.   (**b.**) I'll eject it.

2. **a.** Okay. I'll fast forward the movie.   **b.** Okay. I'll pause the movie.

3. **a.** I'll rewind it.   **b.** I'll fast forward it.

4. **a.** Okay. I'll press *Stop*.   **b.** Okay. I'll press *Play*.

5. **a.** Good. I'll press *Play*.   **b.** Good. I'll press *Pause*.

6. **a.** Sure. I'll press *Fast forward*.   **b.** Sure. I'll press *Rewind*.

Word Work **Partners**

You have the money to buy an electronics item for yourself. Which item would you choose? Who will show you how to use it? What electronics item would you like to buy for a member of your family? Explain why.

Holidays and Celebrations

A **Match the holiday and the item.**

_c_ 1. Christmas   **a.** cake and candles

____ 2. birthday   **b.** costumes

____ 3. Valentine's Day   **c.** tree and gifts

____ 4. Halloween   **d.** box of chocolates

____ 5. Independence Day   **e.** turkey

____ 6. Thanksgiving   **f.** fireworks

B **Complete the sentences about each picture.**

1. This family is celebrating ____Thanksgiving____ together.

_____ is the main course. For dessert, the

family will enjoy apple and _____ pie.

2. Charles and Carrie are celebrating their first wedding

_____. He gave her a big heart filled

with _____.

3. Today is Jacob's tenth _____. He's going

to blow out the candles on his _____.

Then, he's going to open his _____.

4. Many families celebrate _____.

A few days before the holiday, families decorate a

_____ with _____.

On Christmas Eve, little children believe that

_____ visits their home and puts _____ under the tree.

C Many people send greeting cards to their friends and families. Read the messages. Write the name of the holiday or special occasion.

1. A happy day to my special little monster. _____Halloween_____

2. You're not getting older. You're getting better! _____

3. The office won't be the same without you. _____

4. I don't need a special holiday to say "I love you." _____

5. Congratulations on your new little one! _____

6. Today is a day for giving thanks for all the wonderful people and moments in our lives. _____

7. I have so many wonderful memories of growing up. You knew how to make me feel so special, so loved. _____

D Listen to each conversation. Write the name of the holiday or occasion the speakers are talking about.

CD 3
Track 32

1. _____a birthday_____   4. _____

2. _____   5. _____

3. _____   6. _____

Word Work Small Group

Discuss or write about one holiday in your country.
1. What is the name of the holiday? When do you celebrate it?
2. What is the reason for the holiday?
3. What do you do on that day? Do you eat special foods?
4. Do you give each other gifts on that day?

Word Study

After you have a basic English vocabulary, you may want to buy a dictionary for English language learners. Choose a dictionary with clear, easy to understand definitions. There should also be sample sentences for each entry. Many dictionaries have pictures, drawings, maps, and appendices with notes on punctuation, grammar, and dictionary usage. Find a dictionary that will help you continue to build your vocabulary knowledge and skills.

Audioscript 🎧

▪ Unit 1: Basic Words

Numbers
pages 2–3

C. Listen and circle the letter of the correct floor.

1. Where's Dr. Chan's office?
2. Where's the art school?
3. Where's CompCo?
4. Where's the tax office?
5. Where's Dr. Blackman's office?
6. Where's the radio station?
7. Where's the law office?
8. Where's Prime Paints?

E. Listen and complete the forms.

Hello. I'm Jiang Xu.
My student ID number is 354-11-7832.
My cell phone number is 735-555-9480.

Hi. My name is Julia Hernandez.
My student ID number is 555-20-3961.
My telephone number is 908-555-3786.

Time
page 4

B. Listen and fill in the correct times.

1. The bank is open from 9:00 to 4:00.
2. The library is open from 9:30 in the morning to 10:00 at night.
3. The restaurant is only open for dinner. It opens at 5:15 and closes at midnight.
4. The supermarket is open from 7:15 to 10:30.
5. The post office opens at 8:30 and closes at 5:30.
6. The barbershop opens at 8:45 and closes at 5:45.

Calendar
page 7

F. Listen and write the month of each holiday from around the world.

1. Japan celebrates Tanabata on July 7th.
2. In India, people celebrate Diwali in October.
3. New Year's is usually in February in China.
4. Cinco de Mayo on May 5th is a popular holiday in Mexico.
5. December 13th is Santa Lucia, a national holiday in Sweden.
6. South Africa celebrates National Woman's Day on August 9th.
7. April 23rd is Children's Day in Turkey.

Money and Shopping
page 8

C. Write the price of each item.

A. A: How much is this pen?
   B: It's $1.00.
B. A: How much is this notebook?
   B: It's $2.50.
C. A: How much is this watch?
   B: It's on sale for $50.
D. A: How much are these flowers?
   B: They're $3.50.

E. A: How much is this stereo?
   B: The regular price is $125. But today it's only $100.
F. A: How much is the red umbrella?
   B: It's $5.00.
G. A: How much is this ball?
   B: The ball is $3.25.
H. A: How much is this hat?
   B: It's $10.50.

Colors
page 11

D. Listen to the description of each boy's clothing. Write each name under the correct boy.

I have six nephews.
Ben is wearing a yellow shirt and blue pants.
Jesse is wearing a white shirt, and he has blue pants.
Jason is wearing a red shirt and beige pants.
That's Todd with the violet shirt and the black pants.
Sam has a blue shirt and white pants.
And then there's Kyle. He has an orange shirt and brown pants.

In, On, Under
page 13

D. Listen to each statement about the desk. Circle *True* or *False*.

1. The pen is far from the book.
2. The pencil is on the desk.
3. The dictionary is on the left side of the desk.
4. The pencil is between the pencil sharpener and the eraser.
5. The pen is under the desk.
6. The eraser is in the desk.
7. The pencil sharpener is next to the pencil.
8. The dictionary is near the notebook.
9. The book is on top of the dictionary.

Opposites
page 15

D. Listen and circle the letter of the correct sentence.

1. My sister is three years old.
2. There's nothing in the box.
3. She can lift 100 pounds.
4. He's wearing a heavy coat, a hat, and gloves.
5. The baby is crying, and the TV is on.
6. I bought my car ten years ago.
7. Go and wash your hands!
8. He has two million dollars in the bank.

The Telephone
page 17

D. Listen to each sound or speaker. What is happening? Write the number of each sound or speaker next to the correct sentence.

1. (sound of a person dialing a number) - beeps
2. (sound of coins being put in a pay phone)
3. Good morning. Doctor Dean's office.
4. (sound of telephone beep on answering machine) Hi, Sam. This is Sue. Call me when you get this message.

5. A: I'd like to make a call to Japan.
6. (sound of phone ringing)
7. A: Directory assistance. What city, please?
   B: Atlanta. I'd like the number for Costa's Restaurant.

 # Unit 2: School

Classroom
page 19

E. Listen and write the number of each question before the correct answer.

1. Where's the chalk?
2. What's your teacher's name?
3. Where's the book?
4. What grade did you get on the test?
5. Where's Vietnam?
6. What's the homework assignment?
7. What time is it?

Listen, Read, Write
page 21

D. Listen and write the directions you hear.

1. Open your books to page 21.
2. Read page 21 silently.
3. Listen carefully and repeat the sentences.
4. Go to the board and write the sentences.
5. Discuss your ideas with your group.
6. Hand in your papers.
7. Close your books and take a break.

School
page 23

E. Listen to each statement. Where is each student?

1. I'd like a hamburger and french fries.
2. You can keep the books for two weeks.
3. I'm going to call your parents. You have a fever.
4. I need to change my schedule. I'd like to add an art class.
5. The score is 18 to 28. The Red Jays are ahead by ten points.
6. Listen to the conversation between the two speakers. Then, repeat each sentence.
7. It's nice to sit down for a few minutes. Did you give your students their midterm yet?
8. Students, for your homework, please read pages 20 to 24. Answer the questions on page 25.
9. Everyone, take your seats. I can't start the engine until all of you are sitting down.

Computers
page 25

E. Listen and complete the directions.

1. Press a key.
2. Send an e-mail.
3. Click on an icon.
4. Select the text.
5. Open a file.
6. Scan a picture.
7. Insert a CD-ROM.
8. Enter your password.
9. Surf the Web.
10. Attach the cable.

Unit 3: Family

Family
page 27

D. Listen and write the name of the correct person.

1. Who is Hiro's wife?
2. Who is Hiro's father?
3. Who is Hiro's son?
4. Who is Julia's sister?
5. Who is Eddie's grandmother?
6. Who is Yoshiko's aunt?
7. Who is Loretta's nephew?

Raising a Child
page 28

C. Listen and write the number of each statement next to the correct request.

1. He's hungry.
2. He's very tired.
3. He has a new book from the library.
4. He just hit his sister.
5. He can't walk down the stairs.
6. He has a wet diaper.
7. It's 8:00. It's time to go to school.

Life Events
page 31

D. Listen and write the number of each statement or question next to the correct event.

1. We would like to offer you the position.
2. That's wonderful! Have you decided on a date yet?
3. How long will you be in the hospital?
4. When we stop working, we are going to move to Florida.
5. We have tickets for a two-week cruise in the Caribbean.
6. She's beautiful! What are you going to name her?
7. How many rooms does it have?
8. Congratulations! You were accepted to the University of Maryland.

Unit 4: People

Face and Hair
page 33

D. Listen to each description. Write the letter of the correct man in Exercise C.

1. I have brown hair. It's very thick and curly. I have a beard and a moustache and long sideburns.
2. I have short black hair. It's straight. I wear glasses.
3. I have short brown hair. I have a moustache and a short beard. And I wear glasses.
4. I wear glasses. My hair is gray and wavy. I look in the mirror and I can't believe that I have wrinkles!
5. I'm bald. I shave my head two or three times a week. And I wear an earring in my right ear.

Daily Activities
page 35

D. Listen to Eric talk about his schedule. Put his day in order from 1 to 10.

Hi. My name is Eric and I'm a paramedic. I work the night shift, so my schedule is different from most people's. I get up at 3:00 in the afternoon and eat a small breakfast. Then, I go to the gym and work out for an hour. I take a shower at the gym. I go home and do my homework because I'm taking computer programming classes. Then, I make a big dinner and I eat at about 8:00 at night. After dinner, I watch TV for an hour or two. Then, I get dressed for work. I go to work at 10:15 and I work from 11:00 to 7:00 in the morning. I go to bed at 8:00 in the morning.

Walk, Jump, Run
page 37

E. Listen and complete the sentences.

1. I leave my apartment at 7:30.
2. I'm always late, so I run to the bus stop.
3. I get on the bus at 14th Street.
4. The bus is always crowded in the morning, so I have to stand.
5. I get off the bus at 53rd Street.
6. I cross the street and enter the building.
7. I go up the stairs to the third floor.
8. I go into my classroom. I sit down and take out my books.

Feelings
page 39

D. Listen to each situation. How does each person feel?

1. We have a big math test tomorrow. I studied, but chemistry is really difficult.
2. I just worked a double shift, from 7 in the morning until 11 at night.
3. Guess what! I got the job! The company called and offered me the job!
4. I'm sorry we moved here. I don't know anyone in this city. I don't have any friends here.
5. I'd like a tall glass of water.
6. I just can't get this printer to work. I've tried everything! But when I press Print, nothing happens.

Wave, Greet, Smile
page 41

D. Listen to each statement. Write the number of the correct statement next to each action.

1. Look at you! Nice suit!
2. I think so, too. He's the best soccer player on the team.
3. I'm having a party next Saturday. I hope you can come.
4. Adam, I'd like you to meet Sam. Sam is our new computer technician.
5. I'm sorry. I forgot to deliver the package.
6. Hi, Don. How's everything?
7. Hi, this is Jake. May I speak with Marcos?

Documents
page 43

D. Write the number of each question next to the correct answer.

1. What's your zip code?
2. What's your first name?
3. What's your e-mail address?
4. What's your city?
5. What's your date of birth?
6. What's your middle initial?
7. What's your last name?
8. What's your telephone number?
9. What's your state?
10. What's your student ID number?

Nationalities
page 45

D. Listen and complete each sentence with the nationality you hear.

1. Hot dogs are a favorite American food.
2. A French croissant is delicious.
3. You can enjoy delicious Italian pasta in many restaurants.
4. Russian caviar is the best in the world.
5. You can order paella at the Spanish restaurant in town.
6. Brazilian coffee is rich and flavorful.
7. Baklava is a sweet Greek dessert.
8. The new Japanese restaurant has wonderful sushi.
9. Some Indian curries are mild, but others are very hot.
10. That store sells delicious Colombian empanadas.

Unit 5: Community

Places Around Town
page 47

E. Listen to each statement and write the letter of the correct place.

1. How much is a gallon of gas?
2. Three tickets please, two adults and one child.
3. I have a reservation for tonight.
4. Your room is on the fourth floor. Here is your room key.
5. Could you put some air in the tires? And check the oil, please?
6. I didn't like the movie. It was too scary.
7. Please fill it up.
8. Mom, can we get some popcorn and soda?
9. I'd like a room for two nights. A nonsmoking room.

Shops and Stores
page 48

C. Listen to a woman talk about her trip to the mall. She went to eight different stores. Where did she go first, second, third, etc.? Put the correct number in front of each store.

I went to the mall this morning. First, I went to the beauty salon and got my hair cut. Then, I went to a clothing store and I bought a blue sweater. After that, I stopped at the toy store. It's my son's birthday, so I bought him a video game. Next, I went to the bookstore and I found a good mystery. I like to read mysteries. Then, I went to the pet store. I have ten tropical fish and I need fish food. I stopped at the jewelry store and I looked for a pair of earrings, but I didn't see anything that I liked. My last stop at the mall was the bakery where I bought a birthday cake for my son. Then, on my way home, I stopped at a flea market and I found a small lamp for the night table in my bedroom.

Bank
page 51

D. Listen to the information about World Bank and City Bank. Which offers better service?

There are two banks in my area, World Bank and City Bank. World Bank has ATMs everywhere. There is one across the street from my apartment building. City Bank doesn't have as many ATMs, but there is one near my work. I don't like the tellers at World Bank. They are not very helpful. The tellers at City Bank are friendly and helpful. I feel more comfortable there. World Bank gives 4% interest on savings. City Bank offers 5% interest. World Bank has drive-up windows and City Bank does, too. Both banks have safe-deposit boxes. At World Bank, a safe-deposit box is $100 a year. At City Bank, a safe-deposit box is $150 a year.

Post Office
page 53

D. Listen to the conversations. Write the word or phrase you hear.

1. A: Can I help you?
   B: Yes, I'd like a sheet of stamps.
2. A: Yes, how can I help you?
   B: I want to send this letter by overnight mail.
3. A: I'll be on vacation for two weeks.
   B: Send me a postcard.
4. A: Is there a mailbox near here?
   B: Yes. There's a mailbox on the corner of First and Broad.
5. A: What's the zip code for your town?
   B: It's 12817.
6. A: Where are you sending that package?
   B: I'm sending it to Spain.
7. A: When do you get your mail?
   B: The mail carrier comes at about 2:00.

Library
page 55

E. Where can each person look for the information he or she needs? Listen and write the number of each sentence under the correct picture.

1. I'd like some information about saving money for retirement.
2. What's the capital of Turkey?
3. I need some information about whales.
4. How do you pronounce this word?
5. I need a recipe for chocolate cake.
6. What's the weather forecast for tomorrow?

Daycare Center
page 57

E. Listen to this mother's schedule. Then, answer the questions.

My mornings are very busy. I'm a working mother with a one-year-old baby. His name is Ricky. He wakes up at 6:30. He's usually wet, so as soon as he wakes up, I change his diaper. Of course, he's hungry, so I give him a bottle. Then, I put him in his high chair and I feed him breakfast. After breakfast, I put Ricky in his playpen and he plays with his toys. While he plays, I pack his bag for the daycare center. He needs diapers, four bottles with formula, baby food, and, of course, his pacifier. I don't pack baby wipes, lotion, or powder because the daycare center has them.

City Square
page 59

E. A tourist just arrived in this city. Listen and number the places he went in the correct order.

I arrived in the city on Friday. I took a taxi from the airport to my hotel and I checked in. Then, I stopped at the tourist information booth. I wanted a map of the city and a bus schedule. They gave me lots of information! I sat down at a café, ordered a cup of coffee, and looked at the map and the information about the city. Next, I stopped at the bank and used my ATM card to get some extra cash. I also stopped at the travel agency to check on my car rental for the weekend. I spent the rest of the afternoon in the art museum.

Crime and Justice
page 61

E. Listen to the description of each crime. Circle the letter of the crime.

1. I just talked with our neighbor. Someone broke into his house last night and stole his TV and camera and computer.
2. Leo is really in trouble. First, the police stopped him for speeding. Then, he offered the police officer $100 to just "forget" about the ticket.
3. You know the Garcias? When they were on vacation, someone broke into their house. They broke a lot of the windows. They poured paint on their furniture. And they destroyed the lamps, the stereo, and the TV. Their house is a mess.
4. The police caught a man selling drugs on the corner near the high school.
5. You know the big fire in the school last week? The police found a gasoline can. They say that someone started the fire.
6. I hope the police put that woman in jail for ten years. She was drinking at a party, drinking a lot. On her way home, she hit a man who was walking his dog.

■ Unit 6: Housing

Types of Homes
page 63

D. Listen to each speaker. Write the number of each statement next to the correct type of home.

1. I live in a large town. My home is in a long row of houses. All the houses touch each other.
2. I live in the country. I get up at 5:00 in the morning to milk the cows and feed the animals.
3. I attend college. I live in a building with 300 other students.
4. I live in a small town. A truck moved our home to this location.
5. I live in a home on the water.
6. I'm 85 years old. I live in a building with many other seniors. Our building offers services such as a cafeteria and a small library.
7. I live in a large city. My home is on the 20th floor of my building.
8. I live in the suburbs. Our home has a living room, dining room, kitchen, and three bedrooms. We have a small yard.

Finding a Place to Live   *page 65*

E. Listen to Louis's story about renting an apartment. Put the sentences in order from 1 to 8.

    Louis looked for an apartment for several weeks. Finally, he saw a nice apartment to rent. He signed the lease and paid the landlord a security deposit. The apartment will be available on Saturday.

    Louis is going to get boxes from the supermarket. He's going to pack this week. On the weekend, his brother is going to help him move. They are going to load the van with boxes and furniture and drive to the new apartment. The landlord will be at the apartment building, and he will give Louis the key. Louis and his brother will carry everything into the apartment. First, they are going to arrange the furniture. Then, they are going to unpack the boxes. At night, Louis and his brother are going to order a pizza and relax.

Apartment Building   *page 67*

D. Listen to Sheri speak with her mother about three apartments for rent. Complete the chart as you listen.

Sheri: Mom, I looked at three apartments today. I don't know which one to rent.

Mother: Tell me about each one.

Sheri: Well, the first one is a studio. It's small, really small. But each apartment has a parking space. And the apartment building is close to work. I could walk to work. The rent is $700 a month.

Mother: What about the next apartment?

Sheri: It's a one-bedroom apartment, medium size. And the apartment has a parking space. But the apartment is on the first floor, in the back, next to the dumpster and the parking lot. The rent is $600. It's about three miles to work.

Mother: And the third apartment?

Sheri: Well, it's the nicest one, but it's also the most expensive. It's a one-bedroom, large and sunny, in a quiet area. But there isn't any parking. And the apartment is about 10 miles from work. The rent is $800. Mom, I don't know which apartment to choose.

Mother: What's the most important to you—the size, parking, distance to work, or the rent? You'll have to decide.

House and Garden   *page 69*

E. Look at the picture in the dictionary. Circle the correct answer.

1. Is the garage door open?
2. Is the lawnmower in the garage?
3. Is the sprinkler on?
4. Are the windows open?
5. Is the gate closed?
6. Are the shutters red?
7. Is the car in the driveway?

Kitchen and Dining Area   *page 71*

E. Look at the place setting. You will hear eight statements. Write the four statements that are true.

1. The plate is on the counter.

2. The plate is on a placemat.
3. The coffeemaker is on.
4. There is coffee in the mug.
5. The toaster is next to the coffeemaker.
6. The toast is on the plate.
7. There is bread in the toaster.
8. The mug is next to the coffeemaker.

Living Room   *page 73*

E. Look at the picture of the living room and listen to the statements. Circle *T* if the statement is true. Circle *F* if the statement is false.

1. The sofa is black.
2. The throw pillows are white and beige.
3. There's a coffee table in front of the sofa.
4. There are two armchairs in the living room.
5. There are curtains on the windows.
6. The blinds are open.
7. There's a fire in the fireplace.
8. There are two lamps in the room.
9. There's a rocking chair near the fireplace.
10. There's a clock on the mantel.

Bedroom and Bathroom   *page 75*

E. Listen to the speaker. Check if she is describing something that she likes or doesn't like about her bedroom and bathroom.

1. The closet is too small. I can't fit all my clothes in it.
2. We have a large, comfortable queen-size bed.
3. I use the large mirror on the back of the bedroom door every day when I'm getting dressed.
4. There's a new carpet on the bedroom floor.
5. The bathroom is very small.
6. The medicine cabinet has only two shelves. I don't have enough space to keep all my medical supplies and makeup.

Household Problems   *page 77*

E. Listen and look at the pictures of the bathroom and kitchen. If the sentence is true, circle *T*. If the sentence is false, circle *F*.

1. The ceiling in the kitchen is leaking.
2. There are mice on the floor.
3. There are ants on the counter.
4. The window is cracked.
5. The bathroom floor is flooded.
6. The toilet is clogged.
7. The ceiling is leaking.
8. One of the lightbulbs over the sink is burned out.

Household Chores   *page 79*

E. It's Saturday, and Lidia and Luis cleaned today. Look at each person's *To Do* List. Listen to the speaker and check the chores they completed.

Lidia: I've had a busy day! The house was a mess! This morning, I cleaned the bedroom and changed the sheets. I did the laundry. I washed the clothes and folded them and put everything away. Then, I cleaned the bathroom. I scrubbed the toilet, cleaned the sink, and mopped the floor. I wanted to clean the kitchen and cook, but I'm too tired. I think

we'll go out for dinner tonight. I'll clean the
kitchen tomorrow.

Luis: I had a lot of plans for today. This morning, I
paid the bills. I emptied the wastebaskets in
the house and took out the trash. I wanted to
wash the car and mow the lawn, but I
couldn't because it was raining. So, I watched
a soccer game on TV. After the game, I
vacuumed the carpets and polished the
furniture.

Cleaning Supplies   *page 81*

E. Listen to each request. Circle the correct response.

1. Please vacuum the floor.
2. Please dust the furniture.
3. Please wash the dishes.
4. Please kill that fly.
5. Please wash the pots and pans.
6. Please clean the sink.
7. Please sweep the floor.

■ Unit 7: Food

Fruits and Nuts   *page 83*

E. Listen as the two workers put today's prices on the fruit at the farmers' market in Exercise D. Write the price of each fruit.

A: How much are the lemons today?
B: They're 50 cents each.
A: Okay, 50 cents. And the limes?
B: Same as yesterday. 40 cents each.
A: Okay. The strawberries?
B: We just got in a whole truck of strawberries. They're three dollars a quart.
A: Great price! And the apples?
B: Same as always. A dollar sixty-nine a pound.
A: Are the bananas still 59 cents a pound?
B: Uh-huh, 59 cents. But the peaches are on sale today. They're in season—a dollar seventy-nine a pound.
A: And the plums?
B: A dollar fifty-nine a pound.
A: Was that a dollar forty-nine?
B: A dollar fifty-nine.
A: How about the mangoes?
B: They're two dollars each.
A: That's about it. Oh, I forget the blueberries. Are they still a dollar seventy-five a pint?
B: Nope. Today they're down to a dollar fifty a pint.
A: Okay. That's it.

Vegetables   *page 85*

D. Listen to two friends plan a salad for dinner. Circle the items they will include in the salad.

A: I'm making a salad for dinner. I'm starting with lettuce and spinach and tomato.
B: I like mushrooms and pepper in my salad.
A: I have mushrooms, but I don't have any peppers.
B: Okay.
A: How about some onion?
B: Yes. But just a little. Do you have any celery?
A: No, I don't like celery, so I never buy it. Let's see, I have chickpeas, radishes, and carrots in the

refrigerator.
B: The chickpeas are good, and I like carrots. But forget about the radishes.
A: OK.

Meat, Poultry, and Seafood   *page 87*

E. Complete the sentences with the meat, poultry, or seafood you hear.

1. We're having veal française tonight.
2. The special tonight is scallops.
3. I'd like a ham sandwich.
4. A chicken sandwich, please.
5. We're having roast beef for dinner tonight.
6. I'll cook some steak on the grill.
7. I'm going to make meatballs with this ground beef.
8. The pork chops in that restaurant are delicious.
9. My brother is a fisherman. He often brings home fresh lobster.

Inside the Refrigerator   *page 89*

E. Listen to this couple write a list of items they need to buy at the supermarket. Check *Buy* or *Don't buy*.

1. There's only a little mayonnaise.
2. There's a lot of yogurt in the refrigerator.
3. We have only one egg.
4. There isn't much syrup in the bottle.
5. We have a lot of cheese.
6. There are three kinds of salad dressing in the refrigerator.
7. There is a container of milk, but it is almost empty.
8. We don't have any more jam.
9. We ate all the ice cream last night.

Food to Go   *page 91*

D. Listen to each question. Circle the letter of the correct response.

1. What kind of beans would you like?
2. What would you like on your hamburger?
3. What size pizza would you like?
4. What kind of rice would you like?
5. What would you like to drink?
6. Anything else to eat?
7. What do you put on your tacos?
8. What kind of potato would you like?

Cooking   *page 93*

E. Listen and complete the recipe.

To make chili you will need:
    1 onion
    1 tablespoon olive oil
    1 pound ground beef
    2 tablespoons chili powder
    2 teaspoons cumin
    1 1/2 cups crushed tomatoes
    1 15 ounce can kidney beans

1. Chop the onion. Sauté in olive oil for 5 minutes.
2. Add the ground beef and sauté for 5 more minutes.
3. Add the chili powder and cumin.
4. Stir in the tomatoes and beans. Simmer for 20 minutes.

Cooking Equipment *page 95*

E. Listen to each statement. Write the number of the correct item under each picture.

1. Put the soup in the saucepan.
2. Use a ladle to serve the soup.
3. Stir the soup with a wooden spoon.
4. Cut the onion on the cutting board.
5. Put the lid on the pot.
6. Drain the spaghetti in the colander.
7. Set the timer for 30 minutes.
8. When the thermometer shows 170°, the meat is done.

Measurements and Containers *page 97*

E. Listen to each question. Circle the amount each person should buy.

1. How much orange juice do we need?
2. How much soap do we need?
3. How many potatoes should I buy?
4. How many apples do we need?
5. How much bread should I buy?
6. How much soda do you want?
7. How many eggs do we need?
8. How much yogurt do you want?

Supermarket *page 99*

E. Listen to a customer ask about the location of each item. Circle the letter of the correct section.

1. I'm looking for the cat food.
2. Where is the toilet paper?
3. Where can I find dish soap?
4. Where can I get cold cuts?
5. I'm looking for yogurt.
6. Where is the chicken?
7. Where are the strawberries?
8. Where can I order a birthday cake?

Restaurant *page 101*

C. Listen and write the name of the item that each customer is requesting.

1. I'd like a high chair for my daughter.
2. Do you have a salad bar?
3. I'd like to see the menu.
4. There is no pepper shaker on the table.
5. I dropped my fork. Can I have a clean one?
6. Can I have a glass of water, please.
7. I need a soup spoon.
8. Can I have another napkin?
9. What do you have for dessert?
10. Can we have the check, please?

Order, Eat, Pay *page 103*

D. Listen to the story of Luis's first night as a waiter. Then, read each statement and circle *True* or *False*.

Mr. and Mrs. Park are eating dinner at Antonio's Restaurant. They made a reservation for 8:00. Luis, a new waiter at the restaurant, is waiting on them. Mr. and Mrs. Park ordered salad and a large pizza with onions and peppers. Luis poured their water, but he spilled water on the table. Then, Luis served the meal. He forgot Mr. and Mrs. Park's salad. He served them a large pizza with sausage. Mr. Park signaled the

manager and spoke to him about the service. The manager is apologizing to Mr. and Mrs. Park. He is saying, "I'm sorry. This is Luis's first night as a waiter. Your meal tonight is free." The manager is going to speak to Luis. He is not ready to be a waiter yet. He needs more training.

■ Unit 8: Clothing

Clothes *page 105*

E. Listen to each speaker. Number the two items each person bought.

1. I went to the mall yesterday. I bought a suit and a tie.
2. I found a very nice skirt and blouse for work.
3. It's my brother's birthday. I bought him shorts and a T-shirt.
4. I went shopping yesterday, and I got a jacket and a hat.
5. There was a sale at the store last week. I bought pants and a shirt.

Sleepwear, Underwear, and Swimwear *page 107*

F. Listen and write the correct price under each item.

1. The slippers are $23.
2. The socks are $5 a pair.
3. The bikini is on sale. It's $35.
4. The camisole is $17.
5. The bathrobe is on sale this week. It's $45.
6. There's a special on baby items. The blanket sleeper is $9.
7. The nylons are $6 a pair.
8. The flip flops are $10.

Shoes and Accessories *page 109*

E. Listen to the conversation between a mother and her daughter. Match the item and the location.

A: Ready for your interview?
B: I think so, but I'm really nervous.
A: You're not going to wear those sneakers, are you?
B: No, Mom. I have a pair of pumps in a bag in the car.
A: Good. Now, your hat and gloves are on the table.
B: I know.
A: And your purse is on the desk. Do you have your wallet?
B: Yes, I checked. It's in my purse.
A: Where's your briefcase?
B: It's already in the car.
A: You need sunglasses today.
B: I have them. They're in my coat pocket. Now, where are my keys?
A: I saw a key chain next to the TV.
B: That's where I left them!
A: Okay. You're all ready. Good luck!
B: Thanks, Mom.

Describing Clothes

page 111

D. Listen to this young woman decide which clothes to wear. Match the clothes that she is going to wear.

Conversation 1
A: What should I wear with my jeans?
B: How about your pink V-neck sweater?
A: It's warm today. I think I'll wear my pink polo shirt.

Conversation 2
A: What should I wear to the party? I'm definitely wearing my long black skirt.
B: I love that soft pink turtleneck you have. It's really pretty.
A: Yeah . . . I think that would look nice.

Conversation 3
A: What should I wear to work today? I want to wear my short beige skirt.
B: Wear your new pink cardigan. You look good in pink.
A: Thanks.

Conversation 4
A: I'm wearing my pleated black skirt to the movies.
B: Why don't you wear your pink V-neck sweater?
A: Good idea. I think I will.

Fabrics and Patterns

page 113

E. Listen to each conversation. Write the name of the pattern that the woman chooses under each picture.

Conversation 1
A: How do you like the paisley scarf?
B: It's nice, but not with a yellow sweater.
A: Which one should I wear?
B: How about the floral scarf?
A: Hmm. Yes. I like those together.

Conversation 2
A: Which scarf should I wear with this black sweater?
B: How about the solid yellow scarf?
A: No, that's too much solid. I want something with a pattern.
B: How about the striped one?
A: I wore that one yesterday. Do you like the paisley scarf?
B: I do! That looks great.

Conversation 3
A: I'm wearing a light blue sweater today.
B: I like the checked scarf with that.
A: I do, too. But I like the striped scarf, too.
B: Why don't you do something different?
A: Do you think the polka dot scarf matches?
B: Yeah, I think it looks nice.
A: Okay, I'll wear it.

Buying, Wearing, and Caring for Clothes

page 115

E. Listen to each statement. Write the number of the statement under the correct picture.

1. Take off your sweater. We need to wash it right away.
2. Amy, zip up your jacket before you go outside.
3. My button came off. I need to sew it on again.
4. Take off those dirty boots before you come in the house.
5. That shirt is wrinkled. You need to iron it before you wear it to work.
6. Mom, the zipper is stuck. I can't unzip it.
7. That shirt is too big for you. Roll up the sleeves.
8. Mom, where are the scissors? I need to cut off this price tag.

Sewing and Laundry

page 117

E. Listen and write the number of each statement under the correct shirt.

1. I bought a shirt today. A dress shirt with long sleeves. It has a collar, buttons, and a pocket in the front for a pen.
2. I bought a shirt today. Just a plain cotton shirt. No pocket, no collar. It's a short-sleeved shirt.
3. I bought a shirt today. I needed a short-sleeved dress shirt. It has a collar and buttons, of course, but it doesn't have a pocket in the front. I tried to find one with a pocket, but they didn't have any.
4. I bought a shirt today. It's a short-sleeved shirt with a collar and three buttons. And it has a pocket.
5. I bought a shirt today. It's a light blue shirt with long sleeves. It's very plain, it doesn't have a collar or buttons, or a pocket. I liked it because it's soft and comfortable.
6. I bought a shirt today. Just a comfortable summer T-shirt. It doesn't have a collar or buttons. There's just a small pocket on the front.

Unit 9: Transportation

Vehicles and Traffic Signs

page 119

E. Listen to each statement. Write the number of the statement under the correct road sign.

1. You can't make a left turn here.
2. If people are crossing the street, you have to stop.
3. Drive carefully. We're near a school.
4. We are getting onto the highway. The other cars have the right-of-way.
5. We're coming to railroad tracks. Slow down a little. Look and listen carefully.
6. You have to stop.
7. You have to go to the right.
8. This road is narrow and has many turns. You can't pass any cars.
9. You can't make a U-turn here.
10. Follow the signs to the hospital.

Parts of a Car

page 121

D. Listen to a father teach his daughter how to drive. Circle the correct statement.

1. We're coming to a stop sign.
2. Turn left at the intersection.
3. The car isn't moving.
4. That car is going to pull out in front of you.
5. You need to change lanes.
6. It's starting to get dark.
7. It's starting to rain.

Road Trip

page 123

E. Listen to each statement and look at the picture. Circle True or False.

Picture 1
1. He ran out of gas.
2. He pulled over to the side of the road.
3. He had an accident.
4. He is getting gas at the gas station.

Picture 2
1. The driver is getting a speeding ticket.
2. The officer pulled this car over.
3. The driver has a flat tire.
4. The officer is washing the windshield.

Picture 3
1. He's lost.
2. He is looking at a map.
3. He pulled over to the side of the road.
4. He is asking for directions.

Airport

page 125

E. Listen to each sentence. Where is each person? Write the number of the statement next to the correct area in the airport.

1. Ms. Tanzer, you only declared one pair of shoes. I see ten pairs of new shoes in your baggage.
2. I need to see a photo ID and a credit card. Where are you flying today?
3. There it is. That black bag, the one with the big red name tag. Almost everyone has black bags, so I put that red tag on the handle.
4. Please remove all metal objects and change from your pockets. Take off your belts.
5. I need to see your passport. How long are you planning to stay in the country?
6. We are now seating passengers in rows 15 to 25. Please have your boarding pass out and ready to show the agent.

Taking a Flight

page 127

E. Look at the picture and listen to each statement. Write the seat number of the correct passenger.

1. This passenger is turning on the overhead light.
2. This passenger is stretching.
3. This passenger is stowing a carry-on bag.
4. This passenger is turning off her cell phone.
5. This passenger is listening to music.
6. This passenger is fastening her seat belt.
7. This passenger is putting on his headphones.
8. This passenger is finding his seat.

Public Transportation

page 129

E. Listen to each statement. Circle the type of transportation each person is talking about—train, subway, or taxi.

1. I took a taxi to work today because it was raining.
2. I took the subway to work today.
3. I gave my ticket to the conductor.
4. The fare on the meter was $7.00.
5. The fastest and cheapest way to get around the city is by subway.
6. I checked the schedule. There's a train at 8:30 and another one at 9:10.
7. I gave the driver a $2.00 tip.

Up, Over, Around

page 131

E. Listen to the directions. In your notebook, take notes or draw a map. Compare your directions with a friend. Listen again and check the directions.

A: Do you know how to get to Brook Park? I'd like to go this weekend.

B: Yes, I was there last month. Take 37 West. Stay on 37 West for about five miles. You'll go over a big bridge, the Grand Bridge. After the bridge, get off at Exit 6.

A: Okay, so I want Route 37 West and I'll look for Exit 6.

B: That's it. When you get off, you'll be on River Road, going south.

A: So, I want River Road.

B: Yeah. It's easy. You just go down the exit, and it goes right into River Road. You drive along the river for about a mile. Then, you'll go into this little town, Chester.

A: So I'll be driving toward Chester.

B: Hmm, hmm. Go straight through the town; don't turn. As soon as you leave the town, you'll see the park on your right.

A: Thanks.

■ Unit 10: Health

The Human Body

page 133

D. Listen to the directions for each of the three stretches. Complete the directions. Then, write the letter of each exercise under the correct picture.

A. Lie on your back with your knees bent. Slowly lift your hips and then your back off the floor. Hold for five seconds. Slowly lower your body to the floor, starting with your back.

B. Lie on your back with your knees bent. Keep one knee bent. Raise the other leg to the ceiling. Hold the leg with both hands and gently pull toward your body.

C. Lie on your back with your knees bent. Raise and bend one knee. Hold the leg with both hands. With your foot, make small circles in the air.

Illnesses, Injuries, Symptoms, and Disabilities

page 135

E. Listen to six people call in sick to work. Write the number of the conversation you hear next to the correct problem.

1. A: Ace Trucking.
   B: This is Bill Harding. I can't come to work today. I have the flu.
2. A: Board of Education.
   B: This is Ms. Gomez. I teach at Grove Elementary. I won't be in today. I have a bad stomachache.
3. A: Randy's Painting. Randy speaking.
   B: Hi, Randy. Mohammed here. I have a sprained wrist. It's my right hand, so I can't paint. I should be fine next week.
4. A: Mars Cars. How can I help you?
   B: This is Elena. My son has the chicken pox. I'm going to be out the rest of the week.
5. A: ABC Photo. Chris speaking.

B: Hi. This is Lina. I don't feel well today. I'm dizzy and nauseous.
6. A: Harry's Rent-A-Car.
   B: Hi, Harry. This is Jacob. I have a bad cold. I'm going to stay home today.

Hurting and Healing

page 137

D. Listen to the conversation between a doctor and a patient. Read each statement and circle *T* for true or *F* for false.

A: I feel terrible.
B: Your blood pressure is a little low. And you have a fever of 102. Have you been vomiting?
A: No, but I've been coughing and sneezing. And I feel so tired.
B: You have the flu.
A: I thought so. Several people in my office have the flu.
B: You need to stay home for a few days. Get lots of sleep. Drink plenty of liquids, especially tea and juice. Here's a prescription. Take one pill in the morning and one at night. You'll feel better in a few days.

Hospital

page 139

E. Listen to the story about an emergency room patient. Circle *T* if the statement is true. Circle *F* if the statement is false.

Henry was driving to school yesterday when he was in a bad car accident. A witness called for an ambulance, and it was at the scene in a few minutes. Henry's arm was bleeding very badly. The paramedics stopped the bleeding and started an IV. They put him on a stretcher very carefully and put him in the ambulance. They took Henry to the emergency room. The doctor ordered an X-ray of his arm. It wasn't broken. A nurse cleaned Henry's arm and gave him a tetanus shot. Henry needed 30 stitches to close the cut.

Medical Center

page 141

D. Listen to each doctor. Write the number of each statement next to the correct specialist.

1. Tell me about your job. You are worried and angry about it.
2. Can you read the next line on the eye chart?
3. Congratulations! You're going to have a baby.
4. I'm going to put a small needle in your back. It isn't going to hurt.
5. You have a bad cough. I'm going to give you a prescription.
6. You need to wear the cast on your hand for six weeks.
7. You have a cavity in your tooth. It needs a filling.
8. The EKG shows an irregular heartbeat.

Pharmacy

page 143

E. Paul sprained his ankle. Listen to the story. Then, listen to the questions and write the number of each question next to the correct answer.

When Paul was playing soccer this morning, he sprained his ankle. Now he is at the doctor's office. The doctor is telling him to elevate his leg and to put an ice pack on his ankle four times a day for two days.

After the swelling goes down, he should use a heating pad. The doctor showed Paul how to wrap his ankle in an elastic bandage. During the day, Paul should wear the elastic bandage on his ankle. When he walks, Paul needs to use a cane or crutches. If he has any pain, he should take aspirin.

1. What should Paul put on his ankle when he gets home?
2. What should Paul put on his ankle when the swelling goes down?
3. What should Paul wear on his ankle?
4. What should Paul use when he is walking?
5. What should Paul take for pain?

Soap, Comb, and Floss

page 145

E. Listen to Ava's morning routine. Circle the personal care items that she uses.

I have a routine that I follow every morning when I get up. First, I brush my teeth. Then, I take a long, hot shower. I wash my hair every morning, but I don't use conditioner because my hair is very short. It only takes me about five minutes to blow dry my hair. Next, I put lotion on my face because my skin is dry. I apply face powder and a little blush. I don't use any eye makeup in the morning. Then, I put on some deodorant and get dressed. After I get dressed, I brush my hair, put on some lipstick, and leave for work.

Unit 11: Work

Jobs 1

page 147

E. Listen to each speaker. Write the name of the correct job.

1. I have the plans for the addition to your house.
2. I do quick sketches or take photos outside. I do the painting in my studio.
3. Your total is $27.00. Will that be cash or charge?
4. Would you like me to plant daffodils or sunflowers?
5. How large a chicken would you like? Four pounds? Five pounds?
6. What time should I put the children to bed?
7. We have a package for you. Please sign here.
8. How short would you like your hair?

Jobs 2 page 149

E. Listen to each statement. Who is each person speaking to?

1. I'm here to see Ms. Palmer.
2. There's a leak under the sink, and the water is dripping into the basement.
3. My car failed inspection. The left headlight is out and the windshield wipers don't work.
4. Ms. Ramirez, what is our homework for tomorrow?
5. I'm locked out of my house, and the keys are inside.
6. I'd like to sell all my shares of Royal Computers. And I'd like to buy 100 shares of Enerplus.
7. I'd like to go to the airport.
8. We're looking for a three-bedroom, two-bath home in Westwood. And we need a house with a two-car garage.
9. I can open and close my hand, and I'm making some progress with my fingers. I can pick up a pencil now.
10. We'd like to get away for a week, someplace quiet and warm, maybe Mexico or an island in the Caribbean.

Working page 151

D. Listen to each person. What is the person doing?

1. I'm almost finished saving the information. I'll back up everything on a CD. Then, I'll check my e-mail.
2. (Woman singing)
3. Put your hands behind your back. You're under arrest for auto theft.
4. We've put ten sofas on the truck. Do you have any other orders for sofas?
5. This is our top-rated digital camera. It's easy to use. And, if you buy it today, you get 10% off.
6. Okay, Mr. Tremont. I have the information. I'll tell Ms. Georges as soon as she comes in the office.
7. Ms. Paulis, we'd like to offer you the job. Would you be able to start on the first of the month?

Farm page 153

E. Look at each picture and listen to the statement. Circle *T* if the statement is true. Circle *F* if the statement is false.

1. The tractor is in the barn.
2. The farmer is plowing the field.
3. The farmer is watering the crops.
4. There is a scarecrow in the field.
5. The farmhand is working in the vineyard.
6. The farmer is picking the corn.
7. There are two farmhands in the barn.
8. The horse is eating hay.
9. One farmhand is milking a cow.
10. The other farmhand is feeding the pigs. The chickens are laying eggs. The tractor is in the barn.

Office page 155

E. Listen to each request. Write the number of the request next to the correct item or equipment.

1. Please leave the boss a note.
2. Please sharpen these pencils.
3. Please file these reports.
4. Please put this memo on the bulletin board.
5. Please call the mail room.
6. Please correct this mistake.
7. Please add these figures.
8. Please write a letter to this customer.

Factory page 157

E. Listen to each sentence and circle the letter(s) of the correct worker. If none of the workers is wearing the equipment, circle *None*.

1. This worker is wearing earplugs.
2. This worker is wearing safety boots.
3. This worker is wearing safety earmuffs.
4. This worker is wearing a hairnet.
5. This worker is wearing a safety visor.
6. This worker is wearing a safety vest.
7. This worker is wearing a particle mask.
8. This worker is wearing a hard hat.
9. This worker is wearing a respirator.
10. This worker is wearing safety goggles.

Hotel page 159

D. Listen to the conversation between a desk clerk and a caller. Complete the information.

A: Hilltop Hotel.
B: I'd like to make a reservation for September 14th and 15th. We're attending a wedding at the hotel that weekend.
A: What size room would you like?
B: Well, it will be my husband and myself and our two sons. They're twelve and sixteen.
A: I could give you two double rooms, right next to one another. A double is $129 a night. Or, you could have a suite for $189 a night.
B: How big is the suite?
A: The bedroom has a king-size bed. The living room has a pullout sofa.
B: We'll take the suite. What time is the check-in?
A: You can check in any time after 2:00. And check-out is 12:00 noon.
B: Does the hotel have an exercise room?
A: Yes, we have a well-equipped fitness center.
B: And is there a pool?
A: We have a large outdoor pool.
B: Is there an extra charge for parking?
A: No. We have free parking. If you wish, valet service is available.

Tools and Supplies 1 page 161

E. Listen and write the price under the correct item in the hardware store advertisement.

1. A: How much is a blade for this power saw?
   B: A blade is $17.00.
2. A: How much is this hacksaw?
   B: The hacksaw is $24.00.
3. A: Are the extension cords on sale?
   B: Yes, they are. They're $14.00.
4. A: How much is the chisel?
   B: It's $11.00.
5. A: How much is this C-clamp?
   B: It's $4.00.
6. A: How much is the level?
   B: It's $9.00.

Tools and Supplies 2   *page 163*

E. Listen to this order for a hardware store. Complete the list of items.

A: Best Hardware. Sandy speaking.
B: Hi, Sandy. This is Bill Islip from Country Builders.
A: Hi, Bill. What are you working on today?
B: A bathroom. I've got a small order for you.
A: Go ahead. I've got the order form.
B: Okay. Six sheets of drywall and four sheets of plywood.
A: Uh-huh.
B: Two boxes of nails and three boxes of screws.
A: Okay. Two boxes of nails and three boxes of screws.
B: Hmm, hmm. Two rolls of insulation.
A: Okay.
B: Four door hinges.
A: That's four hinges?
B: Right. Just four.
A: And three packages of sandpaper. Medium grade.
B: Okay. Three packages of sandpaper.
A: I'll pick this up in about an hour?
B: Sure. No problem, Bill.

Drill, Sand, Paint   *page 165*

C. Listen to the conversation between two friends. Answer the questions.

A: How is the construction on your new home coming along?
B: Really good. I think it will be finished in about three months.
A: Did they pour the concrete?
B: Yes, the foundation is complete. And they dug a trench around the house for drainage.
A: Is the frame up?
B: Yes, the frame is up. And the windows have been installed.
A: Did they put up the drywall?
B: Not yet. First, they have to wire the house, and they haven't started that yet.
A: How about the plumbing?
B: They worked on the plumbing this week. I saw them cut and install the pipes.
A: Did they paint the outside of the house yet?
B: Oh, no. I'm not sure what color I want yet.

▆ Unit 12: Earth and Space

Weather   *page 167*

D. Listen to the international weather report. Write the temperature and forecast for today and tomorrow for each country.

And now for our international weather report.
Call ahead if you are flying to Poland. It's cold today with temperatures below freezing. It will be quiet tonight, but heavy snow is forecast for tomorrow afternoon.
Australia is sunny and hot. Tomorrow will be cloudy. The hot temperatures will continue, but there is no rain in the forecast.
Japan is cool and rainy today. Light rain will continue into tomorrow. You can expect strong winds.
Beautiful weather conditions are forecast throughout Mexico for both today and tomorrow.

Temperatures will be warm with no rain in sight.
It is raining today in Colombia. The rain will end by this evening. Tomorrow will be cloudy and hot.
France is experiencing colder-than-average temperatures for this time of year. Rain is forecast for tomorrow. Temperatures will fall below freezing, so expect some ice on the roads.

The Earth's Surface   *page 169*

E. Listen to the story of a long drive across the country. Write the nine features that are included in the story.

We went to visit my grandmother last summer. She lives very far from us, and we drove two days to get there. First, we crossed a low **mountain range.** Then, we drove across the **plains.** There were a lot of small farms. Next, we came to a wide **river** and took a long bridge over it. After that, we drove through a beautiful area with thousands of acres of **forest.** Then my family stopped for the night. The next morning, we stopped for extra water and gas to get ready for the road through the **desert.** We finally went over another **mountain range** and down to the **shore.** We waited for a ferry, and it took us across the **bay** to the small **island** where my grandmother lives.

Energy, Pollution, and Natural Disasters   *page 171*

E. Listen to the three conversations. Write the number of the conversation under the correct picture.

Conversation 1
A: Hi, Dad.
B: Patty! Where are you now? We just saw the news about the flood on TV.
A: We're at Aunt Naomi's house. We're going to stay here for a few days.
B: How's your house?
A: We're not sure. The police made us evacuate. The river is rising fast. But the rain finally stopped. Maybe the flood won't be too bad.

Conversation 2:
A: Hi, Dad. We wanted you to know we're fine.
B: I knew you would call us. How many feet of snow do you have?
A: We have three feet! It was hard to open the door!
B: Do you have power?
A: No, the blizzard knocked out all the power.
B: How long before you can get out?
A: The roads will be clear in another day or two.

Conversation 3:
A: Hi, Dad.
B: Kathy! We were so worried about you! We heard about the tornado on the radio.
A: It was terrible, Dad. I saw the black cloud in the sky. I took the kids, and we ran into the basement.
B: How's your house?
A: Our house is fine. But the people on the next block—it's terrible. Four or five houses are gone. The tornado just destroyed them.

D. Listen to the information about the national parks. Write the name of the state where you find each park.

1. Mesa Verde National Park is located in Colorado. Some of the first people who lived in this country built their homes in the cliffs.
2. Volcanic eruptions formed the Hawaiian Islands. At the Hawaii Volcanoes National Park you can hike to some of the world's largest and most active volcanoes.
3. You can take a boat trip through Everglades National Park in Florida to learn about the birds, animals, and plant life in this area.
4. Death Valley National Park in southern California is the hottest and driest place in the United States. Be sure to wear a large hat and bring plenty of water if you visit this desert area.
5. On a cruise of Glacier Bay National Park in Alaska, you can see giant glaciers. On your trip, you might also see whales playing in the cold waters.
6. One of the most popular national parks in the United States is Grand Canyon National Park in Arizona. Hiking to the bottom of the canyon and back up again is a two- to three-day trip.

The World   *page 175*

D. The world population is more than six billion people. The pie chart shows the percentage of the world's population that lives on each continent. Listen and write the name of the correct continent on each part of the chart.

Asia is the largest continent, and it has the largest population. Sixty percent of the world's population, more than four billion people, lives in Asia. Next is Africa. Fourteen percent of the world's population lives in Africa. The population of this continent is growing faster than any other continent in the world. Next is Europe. Europe has twelve percent of the world's population. However, the population of Europe is growing more slowly than any other continent. Next is North America, including Central America. This part of the world has eight percent of the world's population. South America is next, with six percent of the population. Australia has the smallest percentage of the world's population, less than one percent. And what about Antarctica? Antarctica has no permanent human population.

The Universe   *page 177*

C. Listen to the information about the universe. Then, circle *T* if the statement is true or *F* if the statement is false.

The sun is a star, a ball of hot gas. It is the center of our solar system. The sun gives off heat and light. There are nine planets in our solar system, and all of them orbit around the sun in different paths. The planets don't travel around the sun in circles; their orbits are ovals. Mercury is the planet closest to the sun, and Pluto is the farthest from the sun.

Our planet, Earth, is the third planet from the sun. Earth's orbit around the sun takes 365 days, or one year, to complete. Earth also turns on its axis every 24 hours as it travels around the sun. As it turns, the area facing the sun has day. The area facing away from the sun has night.

Earth has one moon. The moon travels around Earth. It takes approximately 30 days for the moon to make one orbit around Earth.

Unit 13: Animals, Plants, and Habitats

Garden   *page 179*

F. Listen to the description of each flower. Write the number of the flower under the correct picture.

1. This large flower has yellow petals. The center of the flower is brown, and it contains thousands of small seeds.
2. This easy-to-grow flower has a yellow center and white petals.
3. There are more than 100 varieties of this flower. It comes in many colors, but red and pink are the most popular. This flower grows on a small bush.
4. This flower grows from a bulb. It likes cool weather and flowers early in the spring. The flower looks like a small bowl. You can find this flower in almost every color.
5. This small flower is thick with hundreds of petals. It is usually orange or yellow.

Desert   *page 181*

D. Listen to each conversation between two people at a zoo. Then read each statement and circle *T* for true or *F* for false.

Conversation 1
A: Here's a tortoise. What's the difference between a tortoise and a turtle?
B: A tortoise lives on land. A turtle lives on land or in the water.
A: That's a really big tortoise.
B: Tortoises can get bigger than that. A tortoise can grow up to five feet long.
A: How long do they live?
B: A long time. Some of them live 100 years or longer.
A: I guess they don't have to worry about other animals attacking them or eating them.
B: No, they can just pull their head and legs inside their shells.
A: What does a tortoise eat?
B: Usually just plants. They don't have any teeth.

Conversation 2
A: That's a big owl. I didn't know owls got that big.
B: Yeah. Some owls are very large. It says here that there are more than 135 species of owls.
A: Owls sleep during the day, don't they?
B: Yeah. They usually stay in a tree in the daytime. Then, at night, they come out and hunt.
A: And what do they eat?
B: Insects, mostly, like moths and crickets. And small birds.
A: Owls have big eyes.
B: They do, but they can't move their eyes. That's why they turn their heads from side to side.
A: I don't see any ears.
B: Owls have ears, and they hear very well.

Rain Forest

page 183

E. Listen to each statement. Write the name of the correct bird or animal from Exercise D.

1. This colorful bird has a strong beak for eating fruit and nuts. It can imitate words and sounds.
2. This bird likes to stand in the water. It can easily stand on one leg.
3. This animal can fly, but it is not a bird. It sleeps all day and comes out at night looking for insects.
4. This is the smallest bird in the world. Its wings move very fast.
5. This colorful bird belongs to the parrot family. It is a favorite pet, especially the green and blue varieties. It has a long tail.
6. The male of this bird has a beautiful tail. It opens its tail and shows the colors to attract females.

Grasslands

page 185

E. Listen to the information about five endangered animals. Check the reasons why the number of these animals is decreasing.

Rhinoceroses are on the endangered species list. First, there is less and less land for these animals. Also, poachers kill the rhinoceroses for their horns. People in many countries believe that the horns have special powers. Each horn is worth $40,000.

The number of elephants is getting smaller each year. Elephants are losing their territory as more and more people need homes. Also, poachers kill the elephants for their ivory tusks.

Cheetahs are beautiful animals. Poachers hunt and kill cheetahs for their beautiful spotted fur.

There were once millions of kangaroos, but their numbers are decreasing. Kangaroos eat grass, the same grass that cattle eat. Ranchers and farmers kill kangaroos because there is not enough grass for all the animals.

Several kinds of zebras are on the endangered species list. Hunters kill zebras for their skin. Also, there is less and less land for these large animals as more people move into grassland areas.

Polar Lands

page 187

D. Listen to descriptions of these four animals. Write the number of the description under the correct animal.

1. This animal has large wings. Its tail feathers are black. It has a black head, a long black neck, and a white area on its neck and chin. Its beak is black.
2. This large animal has a thick body and strong legs. Its thick fur is usually gray or brown, and the fur around its neck and tail is white. It has a large set of antlers.
3. This large animal has thick white fur. It can swim, walk, or run. It has long claws for catching and eating seals and other animals. Its tail is very short.
4. This animal spends most of its life in the water. It comes onto land or onto the ice to sunbathe or to rest. It may be white, gray, or black. It has a rounded head, two large flippers, and a strong tail.

Sea

page 189

D. The ocean is very deep. Listen and draw a line from each ocean creature to the depth at which it usually swims.

Jellyfish like to swim or rest on the surface of the ocean.

Crabs also live near the surface. They will swim down to 100 feet below the surface.

At a depth of between 100 and 200 feet, you will see different kinds of sharks.

At 300 feet below the surface, you will find stingrays.

Sea horses usually swim at a depth of 400 feet.

At 500 feet, you can see tuna.

As you go deeper into the sea, the water becomes darker. At 600 feet, you can find octopuses. Also, a scuba diver can go down into the sea to a depth of 600 feet.

At 700 feet, it's more difficult to see. If you look carefully, you will see squid.

Woodlands

page 191

C. Listen to the description of each animal. Write the number of the description under the correct animal.

1. This small animal has long ears and a short tail. It has four legs. It uses its strong back legs to hop.
2. This bird lives on rivers or lakes. It has webbed feet, so it is a good swimmer. In the fall, this bird flies south where it is warmer.
3. This insect has a long, thin body and four large wings. Its body is often green or blue.
4. This large bird usually walks through the woods. Because it has a big body, it is difficult for this bird to fly. The male bird has a red or orange piece of skin on its throat.
5. This animal is a member of the cat family. It is usually beige and has small, dark spots. It has pointed ears and a short tail. It hunts small animals.

■ Unit 14: School Subjects

Math

page 193

F. Listen to each word problem. Write the numbers and solve the problem. What operation did you use?

Problem 1
Apples cost 99 cents a pound. How much do 5 pounds of apples cost?

Problem 2
A CD costs $12.99. Carmen has a coupon for $1.50 off. How much will she pay for the CD?

Problem 3
George has two part-time jobs. He earns $185 a week at the supermarket. On the weekends, he earns $160 as a housepainter. How much does he earn a week?

Problem 4
Five friends decided to go to a soccer game. Paul went to the stadium and bought 5 tickets for $75. How much did each ticket cost?

Problem 5
Cindy works 5 days a week. Her company is 11 miles from her home. How many miles does she commute each week?

Science
page 195

D. Listen to the science lab instructions. Write the number of the statement under the correct picture.

1. Put a drop of liquid on the slide.
2. Look at the liquid under the microscope.
3. Pick up the metal bar with the magnet.
4. Put the two items on the balance.
5. Pick up the items with the forceps.
6. Pour the liquid in the beaker.
7. Heat the solution with the Bunsen burner.
8. Use the funnel when you pour the liquid.

Writing
page 197

D. Listen and write the sentences you hear. Use the correct punctuation.

1. What time is it?
2. Stop it!
3. I don't know the answer.
4. He was born in Paris, France.
5. I bought everything for the party: the cake, candles, and balloons.
6. I can't work on Saturday, but I can work on Sunday.
7. The teacher said, "You're going to have a test tomorrow."

Explore, Rule, Invent
page 199

D. Listen to the description of each event. Write the number of the description under the correct picture.

1. The United States launches the Hubble Telescope. It sends back amazing pictures of the solar system.
2. China builds the Three Gorges Dam, the largest dam in the world.
3. Alexander Graham Bell invents the telephone.
4. Airbus builds a jet that can carry 800 passengers.
5. The Ericsson Company introduces the cellular telephone.
6. France builds the Eiffel Tower in Paris.
7. The United Nations opens. The purpose of this organization is to establish peace and cooperation among nations.
8. Apple Computer introduces the digital camera.

U.S. Government and Citizenship
page 201

D. Listen to each question and answer. Then, check *Citizen, Permanent Resident,* or both.

1. A: Does everyone have to obey the law?
   B: Yes, everyone has to obey the law.
2. A: Can everyone vote for president?
   B: No, only citizens can vote for president of the United States.
3. A: Does everyone have to pay taxes?
   B: Of course! Everyone has to pay taxes.
4. A: Can everyone serve on a jury?
   B: No, only citizens can serve on a jury.
5. A: Can everyone protest?
   B: Yes, everyone can protest.
6. A: Can everyone serve in the military?
   B: Both citizens and permanent residents can serve in the military.

■ Unit 15: The Arts

Fine Arts
page 203

E. Listen to the four conversations in a museum. Write the type of art that each visitor wants to see. Then, write the name of the correct section of the museum.

Conversation 1
A: I'd like to see the museum's collection of modern art.
B: You want section C, on the main floor.

Conversation 2
A: Yes?
B: I'm looking for the Mexican pottery exhibit.
A: You want section K, on the main floor.

Conversation 3
A: Excuse me. Where is the photography exhibit?
B: Photography is in section E, on the second floor.

Conversation 4
A: Can I help you?
B: I'm looking for sculptures—early Greek and Roman sculptures.
A: You want section D, on the third floor.

Performing Arts
page 205

E. Listen to each speaker talk about a performance he or she attended. Write the number of the conversation next to the correct performance.

Conversation 1
A: I'm sorry I couldn't go on Saturday night. How was it?
B: The music was great! Wait 'til you hear what happened! About a minute after the music started, a cell phone rang. And . . . the conductor stopped the orchestra and turned around. He said, "Everyone, take out your cell phones and press off. When you're ready, we'll begin the symphony again."
A: Wow!

Conversation 2
A: How was the performance on Saturday night?
B: Wonderful! The dancers just flew across the stage. At one point, one of the dancers fell, but she got right up and continued dancing. Everyone in the audience applauded.

Conversation 3
A: How was the performance last night?
B: We loved it! Our seats were great. We were in the third row, right at center stage. We were able to see the faces, the makeup . . . the actors' expressions.

Conversation 4
A: I'm so sorry that I was sick on Saturday night.
B: Too bad you missed it. The music was great . . . the audience loved it! During one of the songs, the lead singer jumped off the stage and into the audience. He started singing to a girl who was sitting in front of me!

Instruments page 206

C. Listen and write the name of the instrument you hear.

1. (harmonica)
2. (cymbals)
3. (violin)
4. (French horn)
5. (flute)
6. (drums)
7. (organ)
8. (trumpet)
9. (guitar)
10. (harp)

Film, TV, and Music page 209

D. Listen to these lines from TV programs. On which type of TV program will you hear these lines?

1. We are going to bring you a live update on the continuing story of the train accident. Our reporter is on the scene. John, what are officials . . . saying about . . .
2. Should school systems remove all soda and snack machines from their buildings? We have three guests today who will discuss this issue, Doctor . . .
3. Kangaroos are one of the most interesting animals. They are found on only one continent, Australia. There are several types of kangaroos, from the . . .
4. Stacy, that was so nice! You shared your toy with Peter. Boys and girls, do you share *your* toys?
5. And now, we have one final question for our contestants. The first person to answer the question correctly will win the grand prize of . . .
6. Tune in tomorrow to find out if Emma will stay with Brian, or if she will leave him for Tony. And, will Adam learn that he has a brother . . .

Unit 16: Recreation

Beach page 211

E. Listen. Check the items that this family is bringing to the beach.

A: Let's go. I have my surfboard.
B: You have your surfboard. That's it?
A: What else do we need?
B: Put the cooler in the car.
A: Okay. What do we need for Stacy?
B: Her water wings and pail and shovel are in the back of the car.
A: I'll get them. And her beach ball?
B: No, she likes to play in the sand.
A: What about the sunscreen?
B: I have it in my bag.
A: Should we bring the umbrella?
B: We don't have it anymore, remember? We left it at the beach last week.
A: We'll have to rent one.
B: Take two beach chairs and three towels.
A: What about your snorkel and fins and mask?
B: I'm not going to use them today.

Camping page 213

E. Listen as a man and a woman pack their backpacks for a camping trip. Circle who will carry each piece of equipment, the man (*M*), the woman (*W*), or both.

Man: I have the camping stove in my backpack.
Woman: Good. Do you have the matches, too?
Man: Yes, I have them. And you have all the food, right?
Woman: I think so. I checked it carefully.
Man: Okay. I have the trail map and the pocket knife.
Woman: I have the compass and the fishing pole.
Man: Keep the compass in your pocket.
Woman: Okay.
Man: And we need our sleeping bags and air mattresses.
Woman: Right. And you have the tent, too?
Man: Yeah, I have it. How about your canteen?
Woman: I'm putting it on my belt.
Man: Me, too. Do you have the insect repellent?
Woman: Don't worry. I put it in an outside pocket. I would never forget the insect repellent.

City Park page 215

E. Listen to each statement. Write the number of the statement under the correct picture.

1. This child is on the seesaw. His brother is sitting on the other side. They're going up and down.
2. This couple is enjoying a picnic in the park. They're sitting at a picnic table under the trees. They have sandwiches and salad in their picnic basket.
3. It's cold outside, but these children don't care. They're going down the slide in the park.
4. This person is a good skateboarder. He takes his skateboard to the park every weekend and practices on the ramp.
5. These children are playing on the monkey bars.
6. The girl is on the playground. She is on the swing.
7. This man is a good skater. His wife just bought in-line skates, and he's teaching her how to skate.
8. These people are at an amusement park. They're riding the roller coaster.

Places to Visit page 217

E. Listen to each speaker. Write the number of each statement next to the correct location.

1. Great! You got a strike!
2. This painting is by Van Gogh. He uses bright, active colors in his pictures.
3. Dad, what kind of fish is that? The gray one with the long tail?
4. It is beautiful up here on top of the mountain. You can see for miles in all directions.
5. Dad, I'm scared to go on the roller coaster. Will you go with me? Please?
6. This is Jupiter. Jupiter is the largest planet.
7. Ladies and gentlemen . . . And now in the center ring, I would like to introduce Zorba, the world-famous lion tamer!
8. We're at hole number 7. We have to hit the ball over that little bridge.

Indoor Sports and Fitness *page 219*

D. Listen to the information about each person's exercise routine. First, write the number of each speaker under the correct picture. Then, write the two indoor sports or fitness activities each person participates in.

1. I play on the local basketball team. We have practice three days a week. Two days a week, I use the weightlifting room. I can bench press 150 pounds.
2. I have a stressful job and I go to the gym every day to relax. On Mondays, Wednesdays, and Fridays, I swim laps in the swimming pool before work. On Tuesdays and Thursdays, I take a yoga class after work.
3. I love ping-pong. I'm on the team at the gym and I practice two days a week. And I just started to take a martial arts class.

Outdoor Sports and Fitness *page 221*

E. Listen to each statement. Write the number of the statement next to the correct sport.

1. The players kick the ball to each other.
2. A player hits the ball over the net with a racket.
3. A player uses a club to hit the ball into a small hole.
4. Players run down the field holding the ball.
5. The athletes run around a track.
6. The players hit the ball over the net with their hands.
7. A player hits the ball with a bat.

Winter Sports *page 223*

E. Listen to the information about each winter sport. Is the sport part of the winter Olympic games? Circle *Yes* or *No*.

1. Ice skating is a popular Olympic event. There are three ice skating events: figure skating, ice dancing, and speed skating.
2. Snowshoeing is a popular winter activity, but it is not an Olympic sport.
3. Downhill skiing was one of the first Olympic sports. Thousands of people watch the skiers race down the hill.
4. Cross-country skiing is another Olympic sport. The skiers race over long distances.
5. Tobogganing is popular with families and children, but it is not part of the Olympics.
6. Most winter sports are individual sports. Ice hockey is one of the few team sports. Many countries send hockey teams to compete in the Olympic games.
7. Snowboarding is a new Olympic sport. The first snowboarding events were held in 1998.

Games, Toys, and Hobbies *page 225*

E. Listen. Write the number of the card you hear under the correct picture.

1. the jack of spades
2. the ace of spades
3. the king of diamonds
4. the queen of hearts
5. the ace of diamonds
6. the jack of clubs
7. the king of hearts

Camera, Stereo, and DVD *page 227*

E. Listen to each statement. Circle the correct response.

1. The movie is over.
2. The telephone is ringing.
3. The beginning of the video has several commercials.
4. It's late. Let's watch the second half of the movie tomorrow.
5. Okay. Let's watch the movie.
6. That scene was great! Can we see it again?

Holidays and Celebrations *page 229*

D. Listen to each conversation. Write the name of the holiday or occasion the speakers are talking about.

1. A: Did you buy the candles?
   B: Yes. I bought two boxes. We need 21 candles this year.
2. A: Are you going to have your annual family barbecue?
   B: Yes, and then we're all going to watch the fireworks.
3. A: What costumes did you buy for the kids?
   B: Lisa is going to be a princess and Stevie is going to be a cowboy.
4. A: Did you visit your mother yesterday?
   B: No, she lives too far from here. But I sent her flowers, and I called her.
5. A: When are we going to buy the tree?
   B: Let's buy it on Saturday. We can decorate it on Sunday.
6. A: How was the party for Ella?
   B: Great! The company gave her a gold watch. Of course, it's going to be strange to see a different person sitting at her desk.